Key Stage 2 Maths

WORKBOOK 5

Numerical Reasoning Technique

Dr Stephen C Curran
with Autumn McMahon
Edited by Katrina MacKay

This book belongs to

Accelerated Education Publications Ltd

Contents

16. Tables, Charts, Graphs & Diagrams   Pages

1.	Statistical Data	3
2.	Tables	4-10
3.	Charts	10-16
4.	Graphs	16-18
5.	Diagrams	18-27
6.	More Data Problems	28-31

17. Algebra

1.	Number Operations	32-33
2.	Arithmetic Equations	33-35
3.	Function Machines	36-39
4.	What is Algebra?	39-41
5.	Substitution	41-42
6.	More Number Sequences	42-44
7.	Algebraic Equations	44-52
8.	Algebraic Formulae	53-61
9.	Algebra Problems	61-62

Chapter Sixteen
TABLES, CHARTS, GRAPHS & DIAGRAMS
1. Statistical Data

Statistics involves the collection, display and analysis of information or data, usually in numerical form. **Data** is the complete set of individual pieces of information that is used in any process connected with statistics.

Data can be collected by carrying out **surveys** using **questionnaires**. Once a survey is complete, a hypothesis or theory can be tested, e.g. a survey on hair colour in the class. How many children have black, brown or blonde hair?

There are four kinds of data:
1. **Primary Data** - Data collected by yourself, e.g. a survey conducted by yourself in your own classroom.
2. **Secondary Data** - Data that somebody else has collected, e.g. a population census.
3. **Discrete** or **Discontinuous Data** - Data made up of certain definite values, e.g. a survey of shoe sizes that your class wears. This is discrete data because there are only a limited amount of values for the sizes in which shoes are made and sold.
4. **Continuous Data** - Data that can take any value within certain restrictions, e.g. a survey of foot lengths in your class. This is continuous data because feet can be of many and various lengths.

This statistical data is presented using **tables**, **charts**, **graphs** and **diagrams** for easy understanding and analysis.

2. Tables
a. Two-way Tables

Two-way Tables can be used to calculate probabilities (see Maths Workbook 4).

b. Data/Information Tables

Data can be presented in the form of tables or lists. They include menus, price lists, timetables, scoring sheets, etc.

Example: This table shows the results of the school rugby team over a three year period.

Year	Won	Lost	Drawn
2008	7	3	4
2009	8	4	2
2010	6	7	1

a) How many matches did they win altogether?
b) How many matches did they not win?

a) Add the won column: **7 + 8 + 6 = 21**

b) Add the lost column: **3 + 4 + 7 = 14**

As this is the amount of matches they did not win, the drawn column must also be added: **4 + 2 + 1 = 7**

Add the two together: **14 + 7 = 21**

Answer: a) 21   b) 21

Exercise 16: 1a   Answer the following:

1) This table shows the prices for child and adult meals in a café.

How much would it cost Mr Owens to buy a lasagne for himself, a burger and chips for his son and a hot dog and chips for his daughter? £____

Menu	Child	Adult
Burger & Chips	£3.50	£5
Hot Dog & Chips	£2.50	£4
Lasagne	£4	£6
Bolognese	£4	£6

2) This table shows the amount of rainfall in three years.

Year	Oct	Nov	Dec
2014	178mm	152mm	159mm
2015	72mm	246mm	335mm
2016	45mm	118mm	83mm

a) How much rain fell in total over the three months in **2014**? _____ mm

b) How much more rain fell in **2015** than **2016**? _____ mm

c. Distance Tables

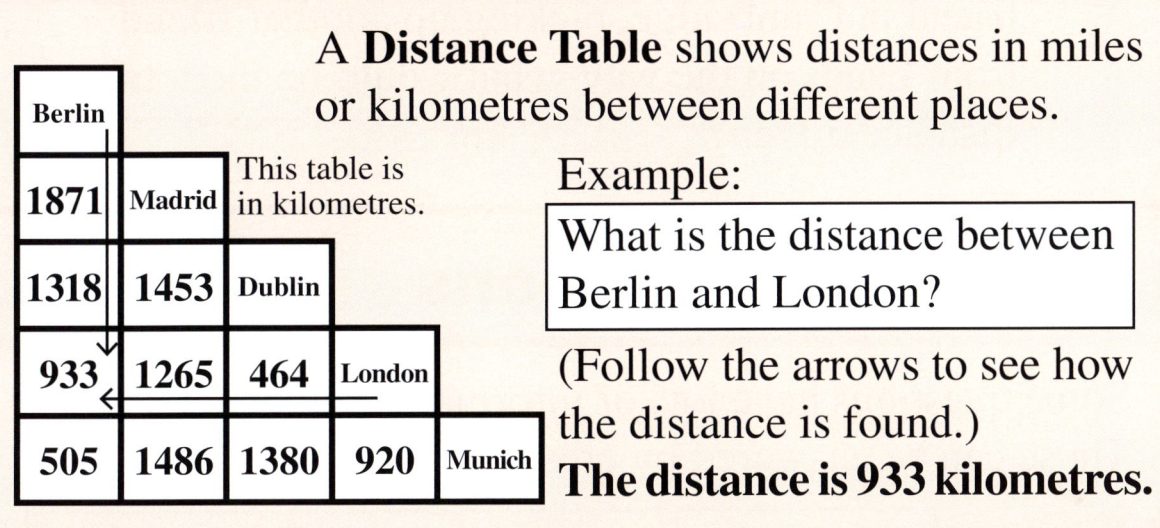

A **Distance Table** shows distances in miles or kilometres between different places.

Example:
What is the distance between Berlin and London?

(Follow the arrows to see how the distance is found.)
The distance is 933 kilometres.

Exercise 16: 1b   Answer the following:

3) From the table state the distance:
  a) Derby to Leicester. _____ miles
  b) Hull to Lincoln. _____ miles
  c) Doncaster to Leicester. _____ miles
  d) If a businessman drove from Derby and back to each of these one at a time, what would be the total distance covered? _____ miles.

4) From the table, state the distance from:

Bristol	This table is in kilometres.			
68	Cardiff			
126	66	Swansea		
333	368	411	Leeds	
272	327	386	244	Cambridge

a) Cardiff to Swansea.
_____ km

b) Bristol to Leeds.
_____ km

c) Cardiff to Cambridge.
_____ km

d) If a student from Swansea drives to see their friend in Cambridge, picking up another friend from Leeds on the way, what would be the total distance driven? _____ km

d. Tabular Questions

Some questions have lots of information all given at once. These can be answered by creating a table.

Example:
A, B, C, D, E and F are six towns.
Towns B, C and E have churches.
A and D have leisure centres and canals.
F has a leisure centre.
Only E & F have no shopping centres.
They all have a town hall.

a) Which town only has a town hall and a church?

b) How many towns have a shopping centre and leisure centre?

c) Town ____ only has a leisure centre and a town hall?

The table gives the answers.
a) **Town E**   b) **2 towns**   c) **Town F**

Town	Church	Leisure Centre	Canal	Shopping Centre	Town Hall
A	No	Yes	Yes	Yes	Yes
B	Yes	No	No	Yes	Yes
C	Yes	No	No	Yes	Yes
D	No	Yes	Yes	Yes	Yes
E	Yes	No	No	No	Yes
F	No	Yes	No	No	Yes

Exercise 16: 1c   Answer the following:

5) Abygael, Syeda, Helena, Saifa and Pheobe go shopping. Abygael, Helena and Pheobe buy dresses. Pheobe and Saifa buy cardigans. Syeda and Saifa buy jeans. Only Abygael does not buy a handbag.

(Abbreviation e.g. **D** stands for **Dress**)

	D	C	J	H
A				
Sy.				
H				
Sa.				
P				

a) Which two girls buy the most? _____

b) Who buys only one item? _____

c) Who buys a cardigan but not a dress? _____

6) Ruby and Riley have dogs. Riley and Marco have fish. Thomas and Marco have cats. Ruby and Marco have guinea pigs.

a) Who has the most pets? _____
b) Who has only one pet? _____
c) How many people have two pets? _____

e. Tally (Frequency or Distribution) Tables

Tallying is an easy way of counting an event each time it occurs. For example, counting goals in a game of football.

Up to 4 are counted as vertical strokes. $||||=4$

5 is made by striking a diagonal line across the 4 strokes. $\cancel{||||}=5$

Discrete data can be recorded on a **Tally (Frequency) Table**.

Example: There are **25** pupils in an after-school activity group. The data shows their ages are: **11, 9, 6, 11, 9, 8, 9, 6, 11, 8, 10, 7, 7, 6, 10, 9, 7, 7, 9, 9, 10, 8, 6, 11, 11**.

Age (years)	Tally	Frequency
6	||||	4
7	||||	4
8	|||	3
9	⌧|	6
10	|||	3
11	⌧	5
Total	⌧⌧⌧⌧⌧	25

The mark frequency is recorded, e.g. **6** years occurs **4** times.
Use the total column to check that all the data has been recorded.

Exercise 16: 1d Answer the following:

7) Find the frequency of the items in this lost property.

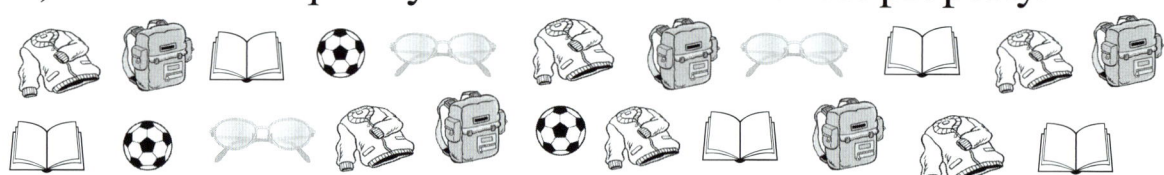

Item	Tally	Frequency
coat	⌧|	6
glasses		
book		
football		
bag		
Total		

Fill in the table to assist in calculating each frequency.

f. Grouped Data and Class Intervals

Data can be arranged into **Groupings** or **Classes**.

Example: Arrange the same **25** pupils into class 1 (6-7), class 2 (8-9) and class 3 (10-11).

Ages	Tally	Frequency
6-7	⊞ III	8
8-9	⊞ IIII	9
10-11	⊞ III	8
Total	⊞ ⊞ ⊞ ⊞ ⊞	25

The class interval is the full extent of a grouping. Here it is **2** years.

Exercise 16: 1e   Answer the following:

8) This is a survey of how long a year 5 class took to complete their homework (recorded in minutes). Using a class interval of **15** minutes, complete the table.

   40, 18, 27, 21, 36, 15, 8, 41, 52, 11, 12, 21, 13, 32, 46, 37, 40, 48, 60, 10

Times	Tally	Fr.
1-15	⊞ I	6
Total		

9) Some students in year 6 were given a spelling test. The continuous data shows their marks out of 10. Complete the table:

   7, 2, 1, 2, 8, 10, 3, 9, 4, 10, 7, 10, 3, 8, 9, 10, 4, 6, 8, 6, 5

Marks	Tally	Fr.
1-2	III	3
Total		

10) The weights of the students in a year 6 class were recorded. Complete the table:
27, 39, 38, 43, 45, 39, 33, 40, 39, 43, 38, 25, 28, 36, 31, 35, 29, 32, 35, 30

Weight (w)	Tally	Fr.
21-25	I	1
Total		

Score

3. Charts
a. Bar Charts

Bar (Column/Block) Charts can display frequency data.
Example:

There are five teams in a league. The bar chart shows how many goals each team scored. How many goals were scored altogether?

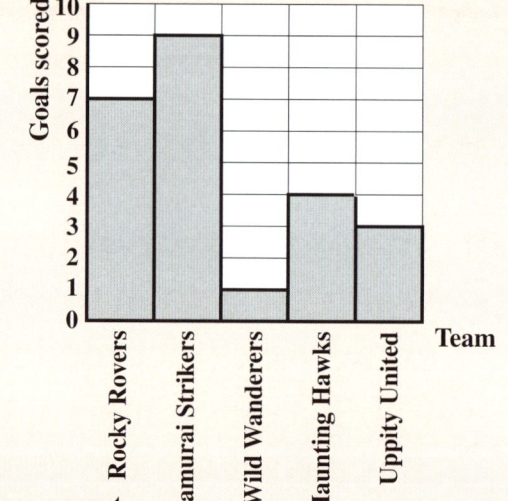

Rocky Rovers	7
Samurai Strikers	9
Wild Wanderers	1
Haunting Hawks	4
Uppity United	3

Add the amount of goals each team scored:
$7 + 9 + 1 + 4 + 3 = 24$

Answer: 24 goals

The same bar chart can be drawn in a number of ways. If each bar shows a range of data, they are called **histograms**.

Vertical Lines

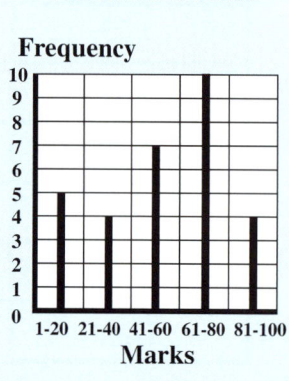

Symbols/Pictures

Drawn Sideways

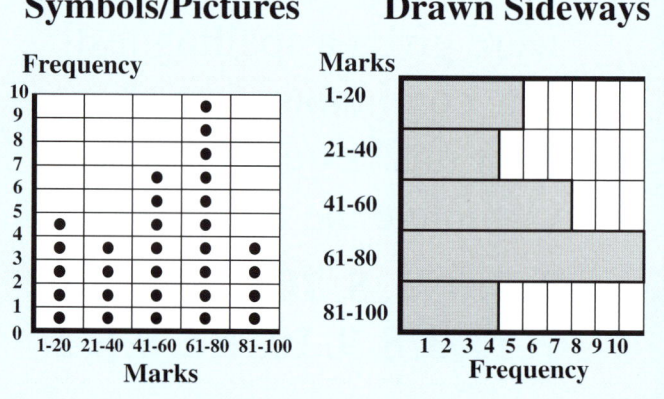

Exercise 16: 2a Answer the following:

1) **30** students sat an exam. Draw in the bars to show the frequency of each set of marks.

Marks	Frequency
1-20	1
21-40	4
41-60	10
61-80	7
81-100	8

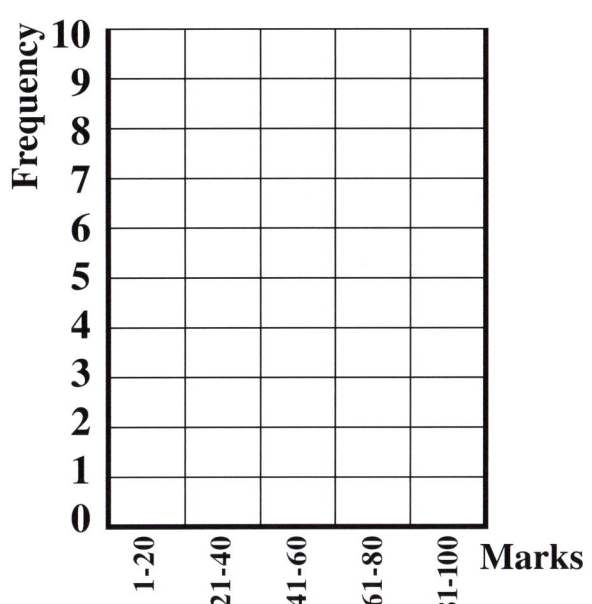

2) This chart shows the number of tickets a cinema sold for one showing over a week.

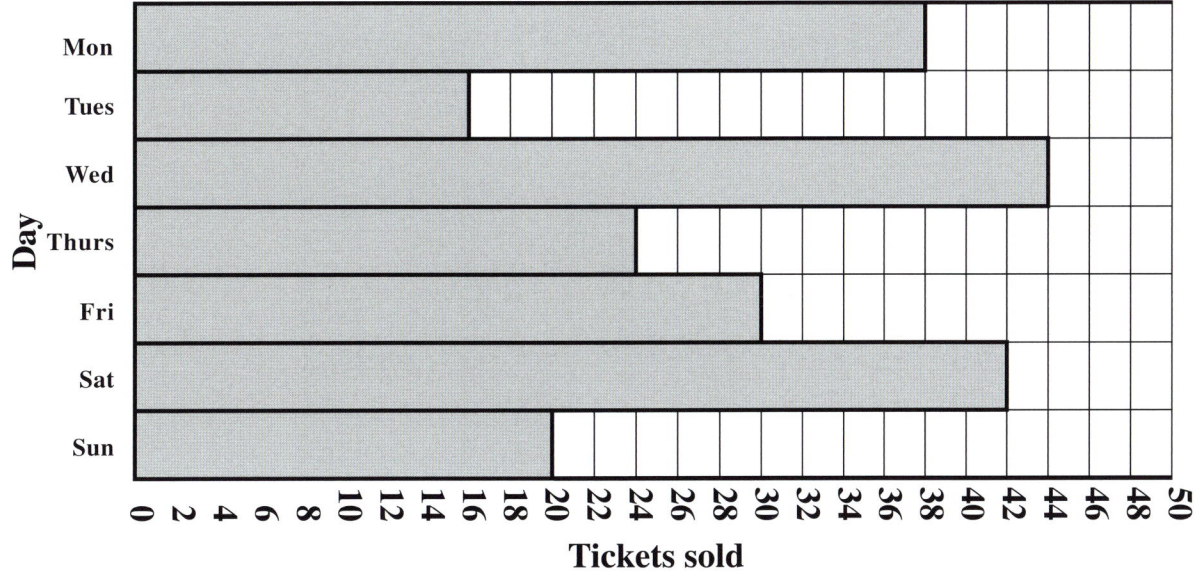

a) How many tickets were sold in total? _____
b) On which day were the most tickets sold? _____
c) How many more tickets were sold on Saturday than Sunday? _____

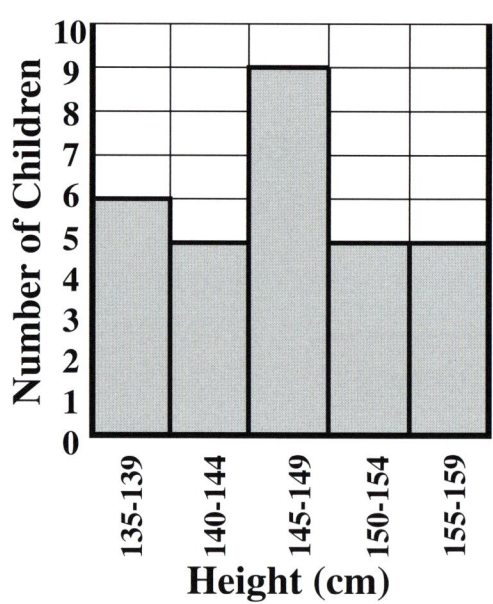

3) The bar chart shows the heights of a class of children.
   a) How many children are in the class? ____
   b) How many children are under **145cm**? ____
   c) There are ten children with a height between **150cm** and **159cm**. True or false? _____

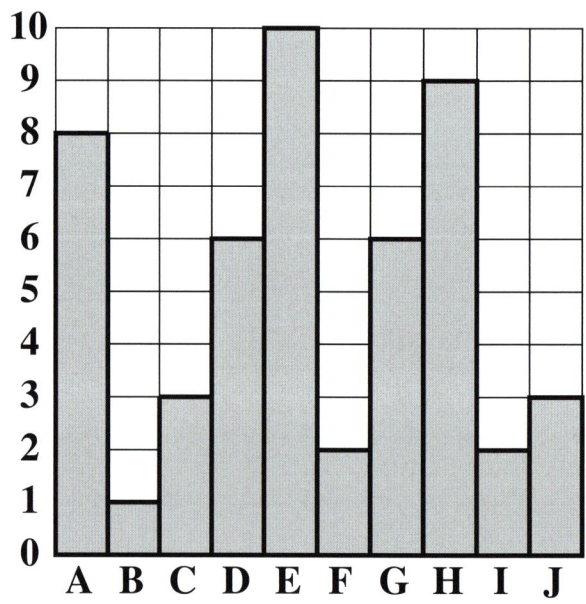

4) Ten teams of children competed on a sports day.
   a) Which team scored the most points? ____
   b) What is the mean amount of points scored? ____
   c) What is the difference between the amount of points scored by team **A** and team **J**? _____

5) This chart indicates the amount of rainfall in one year.

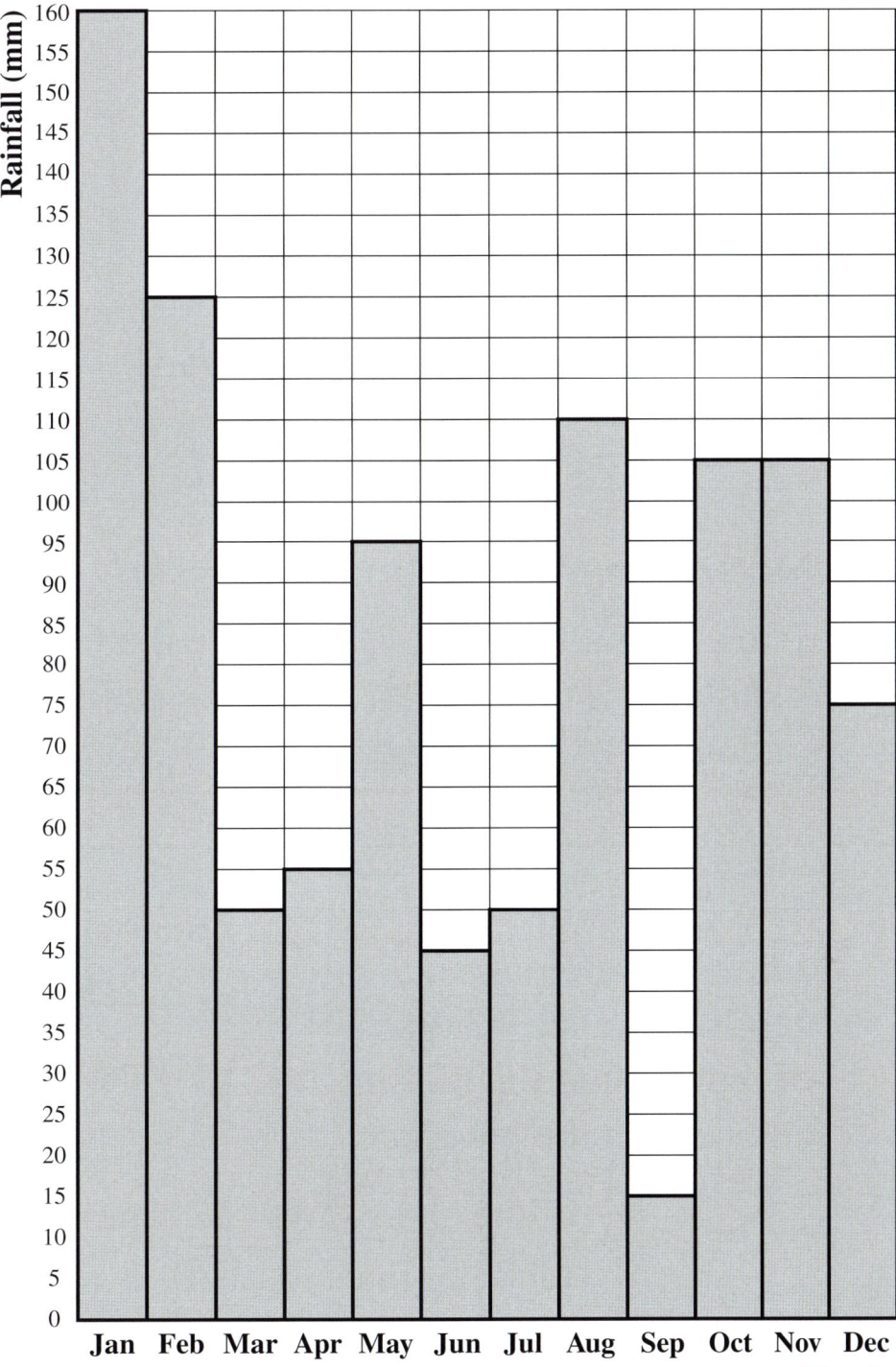

a) Which month was the wettest? _____
b) What was the difference in rainfall between the wettest month and the dryest month? _____ mm
c) What was the total amount of rainfall in the year? _____ mm
d) What was the mean amount of rainfall per month? _____ mm

b. Pie Charts

Pie Charts show things as parts of a whole. Each sector can be calculated in fractions, degrees or percentages.

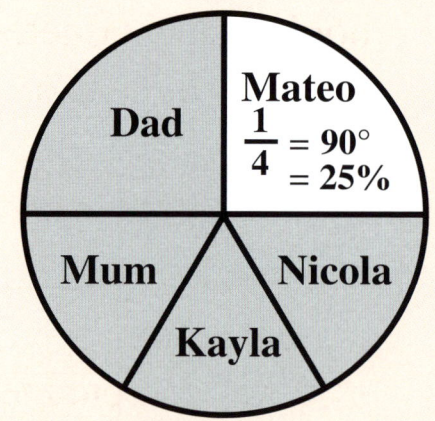

Example: Kayla's family share a pizza. Her brother Mateo takes his share first. What is the size of Mateo's share?

Answer: Mateo's share is = $\frac{1}{4}$ = 25% = 90°

For conversion techniques of the above, see the following:
Maths Workbook 3 - Percentages, Decimals and Fractions.
Maths Workbook 3 - Angles/Fractions.

Fractions are often easily recognisable.

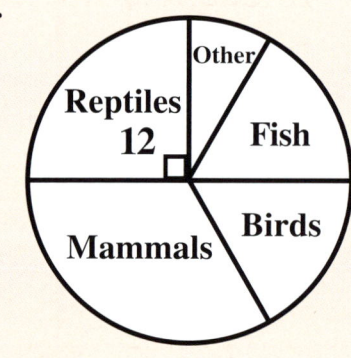

Example: This chart shows the amount of animals in a zoo. If there are **12** types of reptile, find the missing amounts on the pie chart.

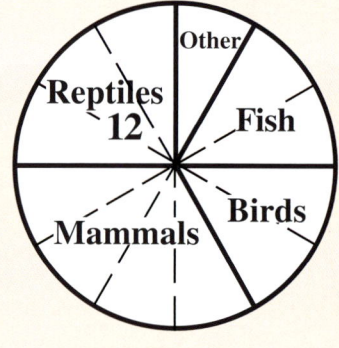

$\frac{1}{4}$ of the chart shows **12** types of reptile. Extend the lines to assist in estimating what the other fractions might be. Then draw in the other missing lines.

The circle can be divided into twelfths.

The pie chart represents **48** animals.

Each twelfth must represent 4 animals.

Therefore: $\frac{1}{6}$ = **8** types of fish; $\frac{1}{6}$ = **8** types of bird;
$\frac{1}{12}$ = **4** other species; $\frac{1}{3}$ = **16** types of mammal.

Exercise 16: 2b Answer the following:

6) A survey of favourite types of book was conducted among **6** children in year 6.

   a) What fraction of children liked sci-fi? _____
   b) How many children liked non-fiction? _____
   c) What percentage of children liked mystery? _____
   d) Adventure is represented by _____ degrees.

7) Francesca has drawn up a timetable for her revision. This pie chart shows how much time she has allocated to each subject. Find the missing amounts on the pie chart.

   a) Maths: _____ hours
   b) Science: _____ hours
   c) Music: _____ hours
   d) Spanish: _____ hours
   e) Total revision time: _____ hours

8) A group of children were surveyed about their favourite treats. If there are **20** children who like cake, how many children:

   a) prefer ice cream? _____
   b) prefer sweets? _____
   c) prefer chocolate? _____
   d) were surveyed in total? _____

9) A survey was carried out in year 5 and 6 to find out what types of transport children used to come to school. If **10** children are driven by car to school, find the missing amounts on the pie chart:

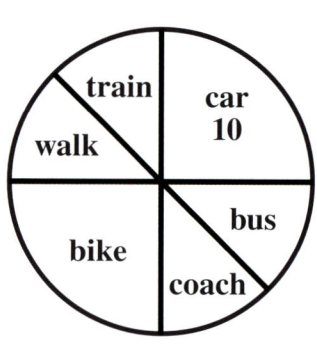

a) walk: ____   b) bike: ____
c) train: ____   d) coach: ____
e) bus: ____

10) A group of **90** children were surveyed about their favourite colours.
How many children liked:
a) red? ____   b) blue? ____
c) green? ____   d) purple? ____
e) yellow? ____

 Score

4. Graphs
a. Line Graphs

A **Line Graph** is similar to a bar chart. Points are plotted in the middle of the class intervals (see Circles). If straight lines are used between points it is also called a **frequency polygon**.

Example:

Plot the points and draw the line graph.

Speed	Frequency
0-20	3
21-40	8
41-60	10
61-80	4
81-100	2

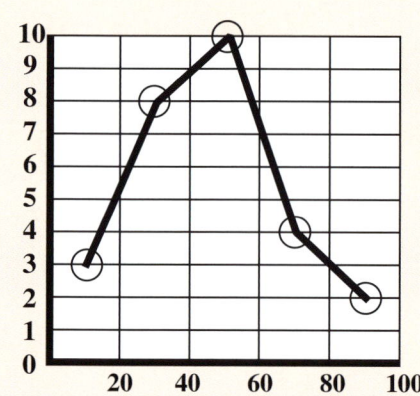

Exercise 16: 3   Answer the following:

The graph shows the temperatures in London over a week.

1) What day was hottest? _____

2) What day was coolest? _____

3) What is the range of temperatures? _____

4) What is the mean of the temperatures? _____

5) Which two days were the same temperature?
   _____ & _____

The results of a science exam are shown in this table:

Score (%)	Fr
1-10	2
11-20	5
21-30	6
31-40	4
41-50	7
51-60	10
61-70	9
71-80	11
81-90	15
91-100	8

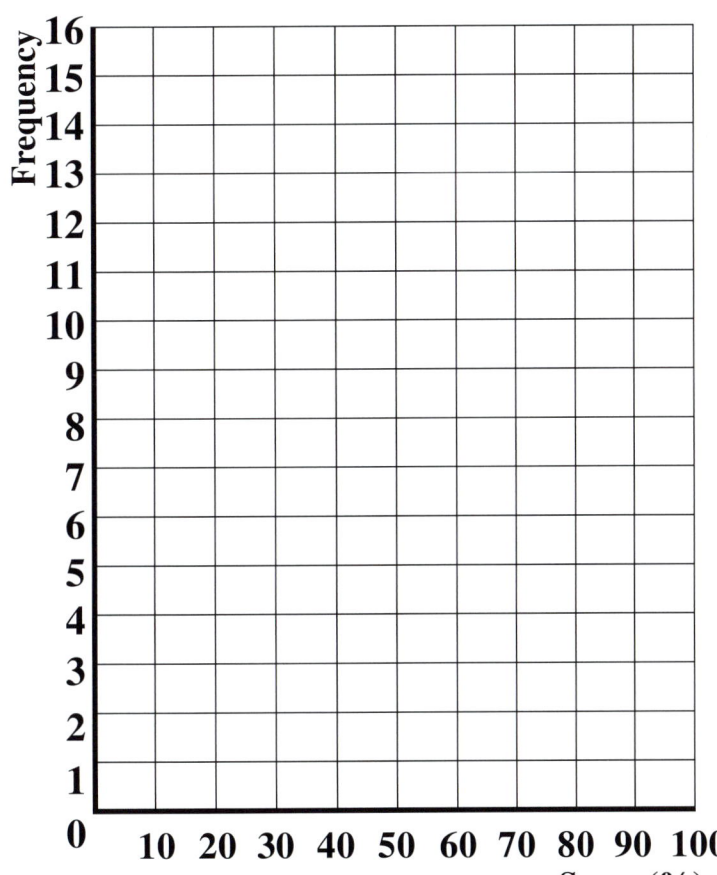

6) Draw a line graph of the information.

7) How many students took the exam? _____

8) What percentage interval did the most pupils score? _____

9) What percentage interval did the fewest pupils score? _____

10) If the pass mark was **51%** how many students passed? _____

Score

5. Diagrams
a. Pictograms

In **Pictograms** pictures represent a certain number of items.

Example: A postman kept track of the amount of letters he delivered in one week.
a) How many did he deliver altogether?
b) How many did he deliver on Tuesday?

✉ = **10** letters   ✉ = **5** letters

Mon	✉✉✉
Tue	✉✉
Wed	✉✉
Thu	✉✉✉
Fri	✉✉

Answers:
a) **110**
b) **20**

Exercise 16: 4   Answer the following:

Some sweets were shared out between **5** girls.

🍬 - 4 sweets   🍬 - 2 sweets

Isobella   🍬
Vickie   🍬 🍬
Marian   🍬 🍬 🍬
Zainab   🍬
Roseanne   🍬 🍬

1) How many sweets were shared? _____
2) Who received the most sweets? _____
3) Who received the least sweets? _____
4) How many sweets did Roseanne receive? _____
5) Who received **2** more sweets than Zainab? _____

This shows the number of hours of sunshine for a week in August.

☀ = **2** hours   ☼ = **1** hour

Mon	☀ ☀ ☀ ☀ ☀ ☀ ☀ ☼
Tue	☀ ☀ ☀ ☀ ☀ ☀ ☼
Wed	☀ ☀ ☀ ☀ ☀
Thu	☀ ☀ ☀ ☀ ☀ ☀ ☼
Fri	☀ ☀ ☀ ☀ ☀
Sat	☀ ☀ ☼
Sun	☀ ☼

6) Which day has the most hours of sunshine? _____
7) Which day has the least hours of sunshine? _____
8) Which day has **5** hours of sunshine? _____
9) Which day has **2** more hours of sunshine than Thursday? _____
10) How many hours of sunshine were there in total? _____ hours

Score

b. Venn Diagrams
(i) Set and Venn Diagram Rules

A **Venn Diagram** is used to sort data into groups or **sets**. A set is a collection of things that belong together.

A Venn diagram shows the relationship between different sets, which are collected together using circles which can overlap or **intersect**.

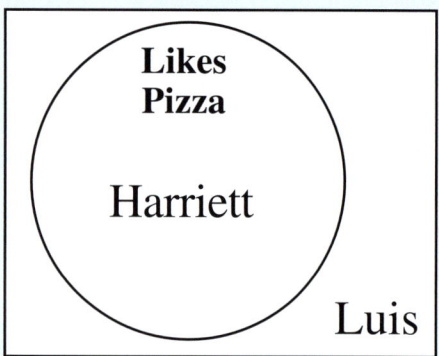

This Venn diagram shows that Harriett likes pizza as she is within the 'likes pizza' circle. As Luis is outside this circle, it means he does not like pizza.

This Venn diagram shows that Harriett likes pizza and Luis likes Chocolate.

Jai is in the intersection between pizza and chocolate, meaning he likes both.

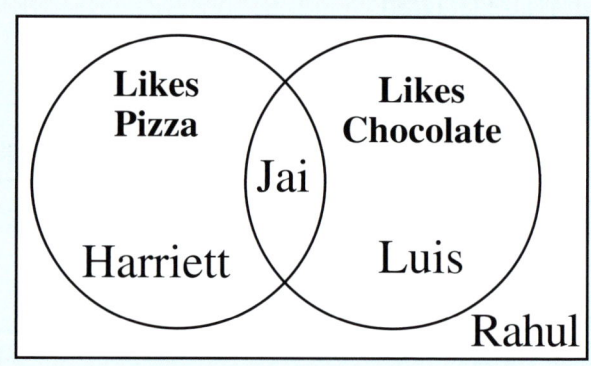

Rahul is outside both circles, meaning he does not like pizza or chocolate.

Example: Insert these values into the Venn diagram.
1, 2, 3, 6, 7, 9, 18, 21, 27

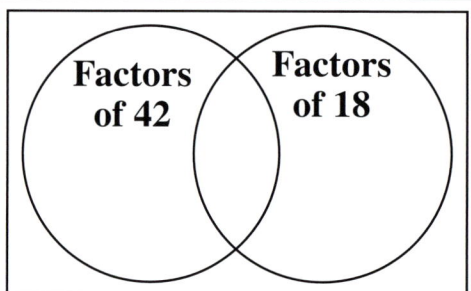

Step 1 - Sort the factors of **42**. These are **1, 2, 3, 6, 7, 21** and **42**.

Step 2 - Sort the factors of **18**. These are **1, 2, 3, 6, 9** and **18**.

Step 3 - **1, 2, 3** and **6** are factors of both numbers, so these numbers will go in the intersection.

Step 4 - **27** is not a factor of either **42** or **18**, so this will be positioned outside the circles.

Answer: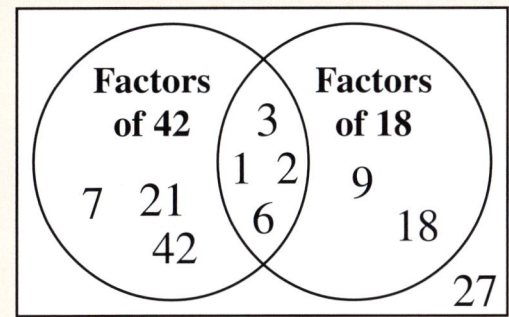

Exercise 16: 5

Insert the values into the Venn diagram:

1-7) 1   3
     10 28
      7   2
     20

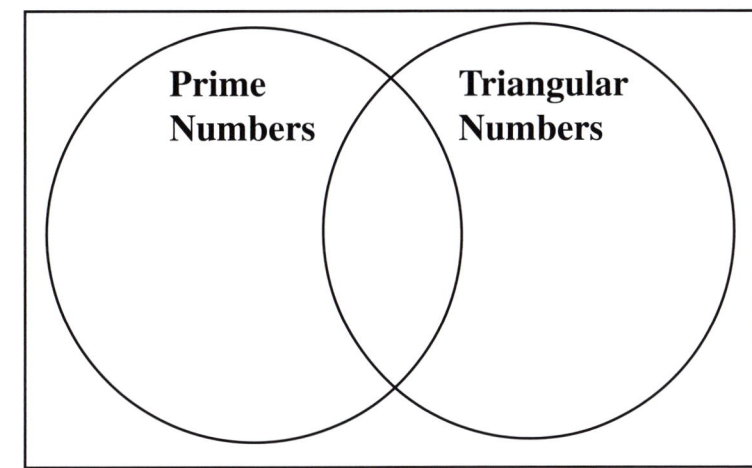

8) Which number(s) belong in the overlap? _____

9) Which number(s) do not belong in a circle? _____

10) Which number(s) only belong in the prime numbers circle? _____

Exercise 16: 6   Insert the values into the Venn diagram:

Score

1-8) 1   4
      9   10
      15 25
      8   17

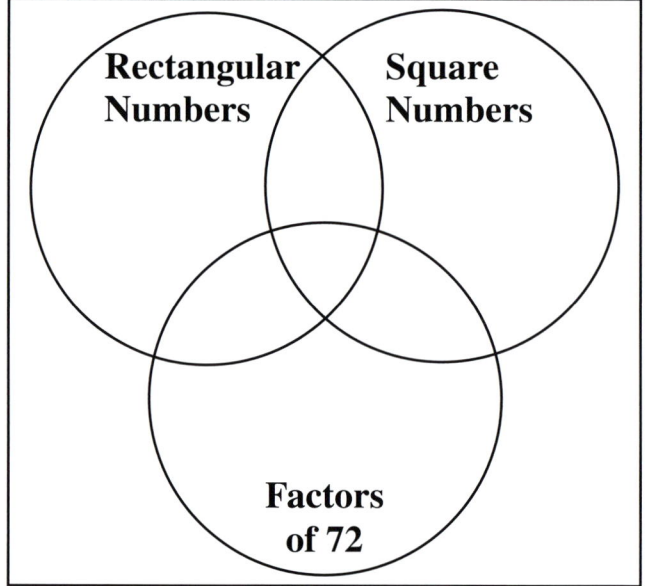

9) Which number(s) belong(s) in the rectangular numbers section only? _____

10) Which number(s) do(es) not belong in the circles? _____

(ii) Sets and Carroll Diagrams

A **Carroll Diagram**, although seen less frequently, is an alternative way of sorting things into various groups or sets. It is named after the famous children's author Lewis Carroll who wrote *Alice in Wonderland*.

Example: | Sort the different shapes into four basic sets using black and white as the main criteria of grouping.

The basic groupings would be black/white and then odd/even can also be used as follows:

	Odd numbered sides	Even numbered sides
Black		
White		

Exercise 16: 7

Sort the numbers into the Carroll diagram:

Score

1) 9
2) 15
3) 12
4) 49
5) 14
6) 35
7) 70
8) 36
9) 27
10) 28

	Multiples of 3	Multiples of 7
Odd		
Even		

© 2018 Stephen Curran

Exercise 16: 8

Sort the numbers into the Carroll diagram:

Score

1) 2
2) 21
3) 20
4) 5
5) 8
6) 4
7) 3
8) 7
9) 40
10) 10

	Prime	Not Prime
Factors of 40		
Factors of 21		

c. Mappings

A **Mapping** (or function) is a connection between two sets. Each first set member links with a second set member.

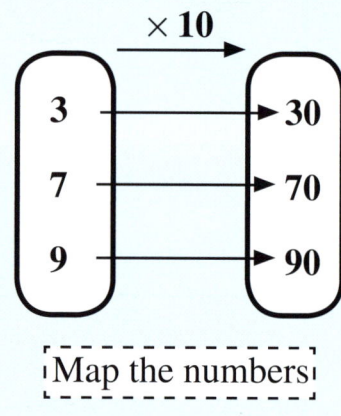

Map the numbers

Examples:
Note that members of the first set here have only one partner but the second set can have more.

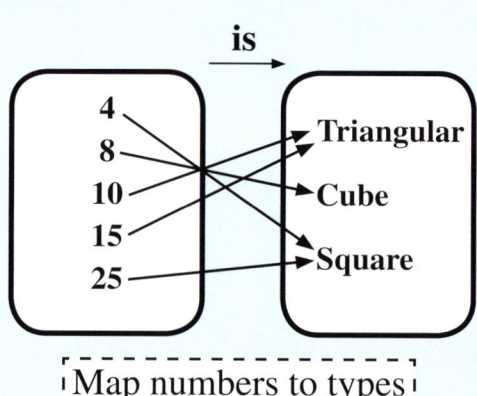

Map numbers to types

Mappings often make use of the Four Rules of Number. They can have two operations.
Test them out using: $+ - \times \div$

24 © 2018 Stephen Curran

Exercise 16: 9a Do the following mappings:

1) Write in the mapping rule: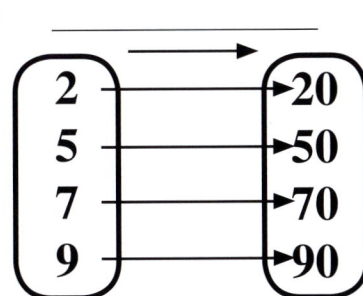

2) Draw in the arrows for these mappings: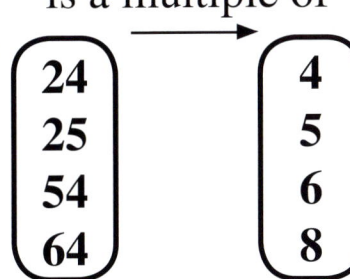

is a multiple of

3) Write in the mapping rule: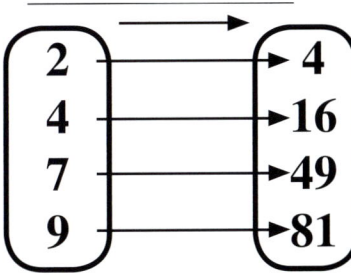

4) Write in the missing numbers: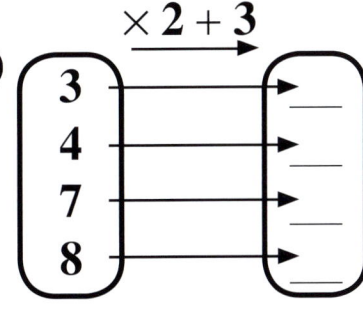

5) Work out the mapping rule and write in the missing number: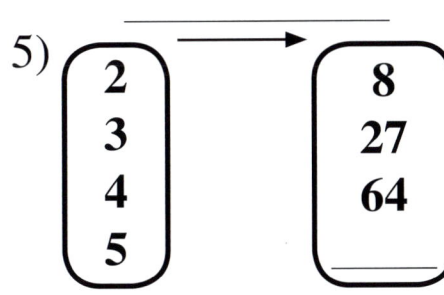

6) Work out the mapping rule and write in the missing number: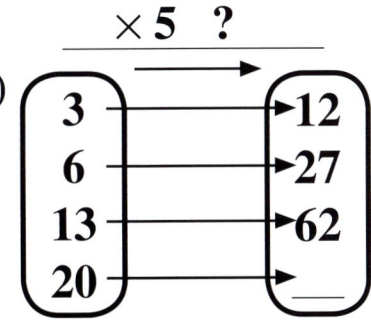

d. Flow Diagrams

Flow Diagrams or **decision trees** provide a process for items to be classified or sorted into various groups.

Example:

| Make up a decision tree to help Daniel sort out a pile of textbooks and workbooks. |

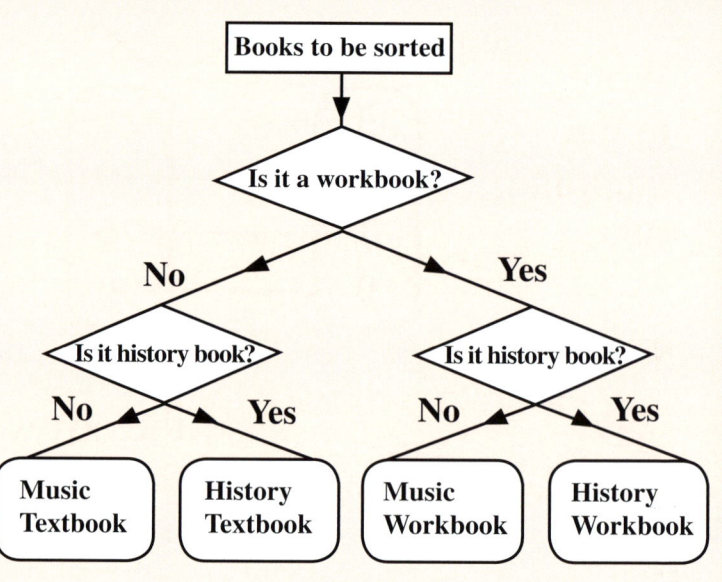

A **family tree** is another type of flow diagram.

Example:

| This family tree shows three generations of the Murphy family. Who is Jennifer's grandfather? |

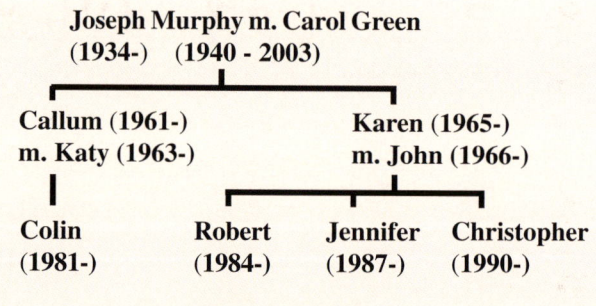

m. means married

Answer: Joseph Murphy

Exercise 16: 9b   Answer the following:

7) Use the same Murphy family tree (above) to answer:
   a) How old was Callum when his son Colin was born?
   _____ yrs
   b) Christopher is Callum's _____ .
   c) Jennifer is Robert's _____ .
   d) How old was Robert when his grandmother died?
   _____ yrs

8) A flow diagram is drawn to classify four shapes.

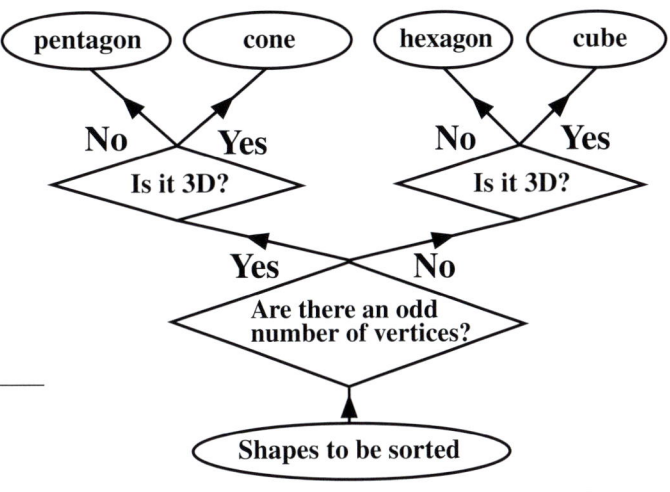

a) Which shape is 3D and has an odd number of vertices? _____

b) Which shape is not 3D and has not got an odd number of vertices? _____

c) A cube is 3D, true or false? _____

e. Relational Diagrams

A **Relational Diagram** can help solve a problem where things relate to each other.
Example:

In **5** years' time, Stuart will be three times as old as his sister is now. His sister is **5** years old. How old is Stuart now?

5 × 3 = 15 years
15 − 5 = 10 years

Answer: Stuart is **10** years old.

Exercise 16: 9c   Answer the following:

9) Clare is **6cm** taller than Sofia who is **11cm** shorter than Stephan. Who is the tallest? _____

10) Seven years ago, Denis was **4** years old. His mother was six times his age.
    a) How old is his mother now? ____ years
    b) How old is Dennis now? ____ years

Score

6. More Data Problems

Exercise 16: 10   Answer the following:

1) A group of people were surveyed about how they travelled to work. If **60** people were surveyed in total, find the missing amounts on the pie chart.

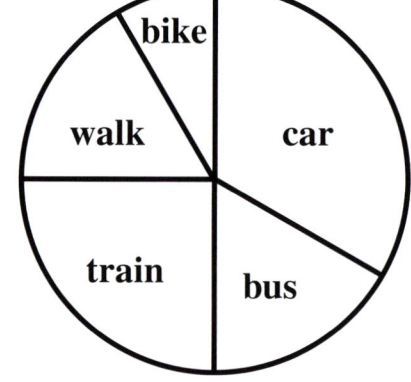

   a) bike: ____   b) car: ____
   c) bus: ____   d) train: ____
   e) walk: ____

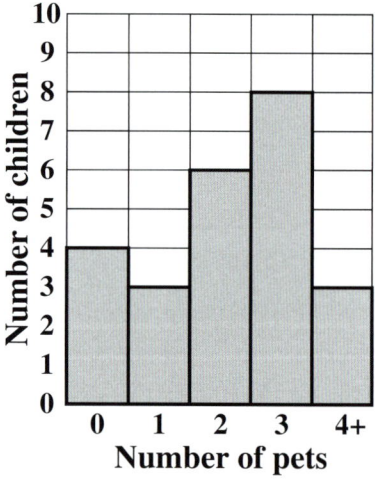

2) A class of year 6 children were surveyed about the number of pets they owned. The bar chart shows the results. How many children were surveyed in total? ____

3) This chart shows the favourite type of book of a class of students. There are **30** students in the class. How many children like all three types of book? ____

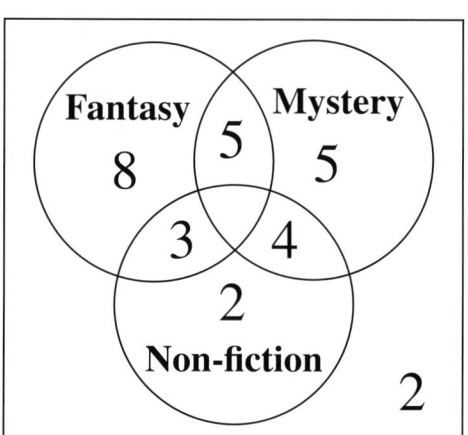

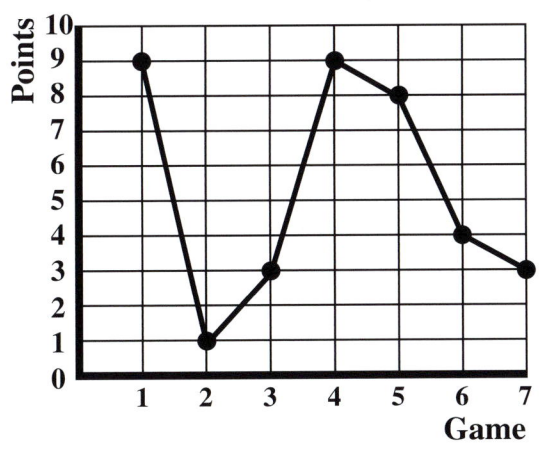

4) This shows the number of points Enrico scored over 7 games on his computer. What is the range of his scores? ____

5) Using this table, draw the missing bars on the chart.

Holiday Destination	Frequency
Menorca	5
Barbados	2
USA	10
Cornwall	3
Sydney	2

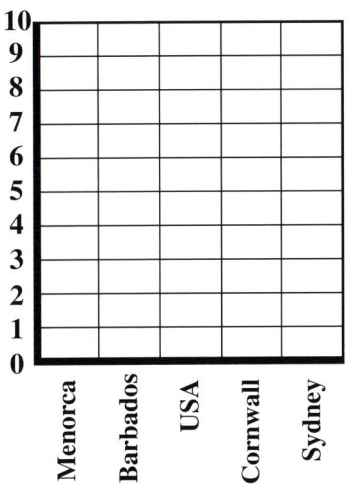

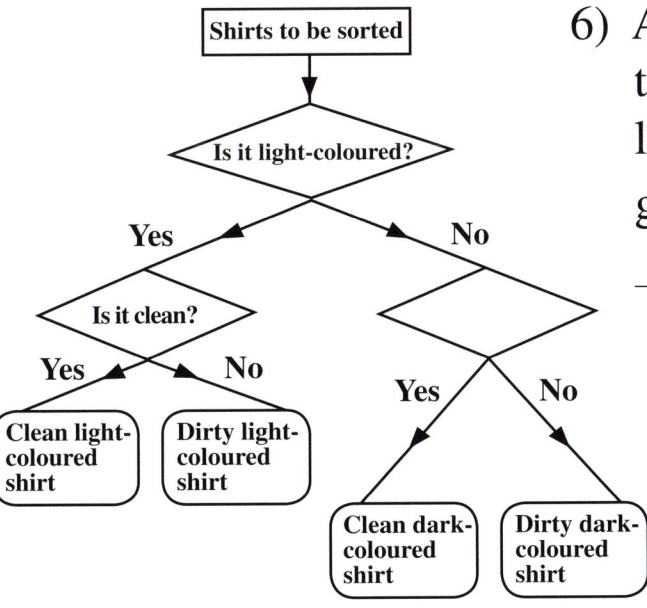

6) A flow diagram is drawn to help Caitlin sort out her laundry. What question goes in the blank space?

_____

7) This pictogram shows how many goals some teams scored in the first round of the Football World Cup.

⚽ = 2 goals   ◖ = 1 goal

Russia	⚽ ⚽ ⚽ ⚽
Portugal	⚽ ⚽ ◖
England	⚽ ⚽ ⚽ ⚽ ⚽
Belgium	⚽ ⚽ ⚽ ⚽ ⚽
Tunisia	⚽ ◖

How many goals were scored in total? _____

8) Put the following numbers in this Carroll diagram:

3   5   6   8   10   12   20   40

	Factors of 12	Factors of 40
Odd		
Even		

30 © 2018 Stephen Curran

9) This table shows how many matches some teams in one group won in the Rugby World Cup.

Team	Won	Lost	Drawn
Ireland	1	2	0
New Zealand	1	1	1
Japan	1	0	2
Uruguay	1	1	1

a) Which team lost the most games? _____
b) How many games did Uruguay not win? ____
c) Which team performed the best? _____

10) This table is in miles.

Wolverhampton				
40	Worcester			
151	156	Basildon		
148	146	69	Guildford	
43	75	154	150	Derby

From the table, state the distance:
a) Wolverhampton to Derby. ____ miles
b) Basildon to Guildford. ____ miles
c) Worcester to Guildford. ____ miles

Score

Chapter Seventeen
ALGEBRA
1. Number Operations
a. BIDMAS (BODMAS)

BIDMAS is an acronym which helps to remind us of the order certain operations have to follow:

B I D M A S

Brackets, **I**ndices, **D**ivide, **M**ultiply, **A**dd, **S**ubtract

Order of Operations is as follows:
1. Do anything in **Brackets**.
2. Do anything with **Indices** (or **Orders** - another word for powers).
3. Do any **Dividing** or **Multiplying** (in the order of the question).
4. Do any **Adding** or **Subtracting** (in the order of the question).

Example: Work out the following sum using BIDMAS:

$\dfrac{18}{(8+1)} \times (4+2+5)^2 - 10$

1. Work out the brackets first:
   a. $(8+1) = 9$
   b. $(4+2+5)^2 = 11^2 = 121$

$\dfrac{18}{9} \times 121 - 10$

2. Next work out the division and then the multiplication:
   $18 \div 9 = 2$; $2 \times 121 = 242$

$2 \times 121 - 10$

$242 - 10$

3. Now do the subtraction:
   $242 - 10 = 232$

232 (answer)

Exercise 17: 1 Calculate the following: Score

The two sums are treated as bracketed.

1) $(47 - 14) \times 2 + 16$

= _____

2) $\dfrac{45 - 17}{7 \times 2} \longrightarrow \dfrac{(45 - 17)}{(7 \times 2)}$

= _____

3) $(11 \times 12) + (1 \times 8)^2$

= _____

4) $6(10 + 6) + 4$

= _____

5) $(5 \times 7) + (10 \times 2) + (6 \times 2)^2 =$ _____

6) $5(8 + 8) - 4$

= _____

7) $(9^2 + 3^2) - (10 - 4)^2$

= _____

8) $3(4 - 2) + (\text{-}10 - 8) + (7 \times 1)^2 =$ _____

9) $\dfrac{(8 \times 1)}{(10 - 6)} + 26 =$ _____

10) $9(6 + 2) - 29$

= _____

2. Arithmetic Equations

Equations are mathematical sentences or number sentences that always follow the same pattern. What is on the left side is **balanced** or **equal to** what is on the right side of the equals sign. This is always signified by an **equals sign**.

Examples: Show equations using the four rules of number.

Both equations remain balanced giving the same answer on each side.

$9 - 4 = 3 + 2$
$5 = 5$

$6 \times 2 = 48 \div 4$
$12 = 12$

a. Missing Numbers

The equals sign permits a **Missing Number** to be found. Inverse operations can be used to solve the equations. Remember: + is the inverse of − and × is the inverse of ÷

Examples: Find the missing numbers in these equations:

$\boxed{?} + 8 = 15$ The number in the box is **7** because:
$\boxed{7} + 8 = 15$ (inverted $\boxed{7} = 15 - 8$)

$8 \times \boxed{?} = 16$ The number in the box is **2** because:
$8 \times \boxed{2} = 16$ (inverted $\boxed{2} = 16 \div 8$)

Exercise 17: 2a   Calculate the following:

1) $\boxed{} + 4 = 37$

2) $97 - 85 = \boxed{} - 4$

3) $64 + 36 = 86 + \boxed{}$

4) $\boxed{} + 17 = 41 + 6$

5) $93 - \boxed{} = 19$

6) $(80 \div 8) - 9 = \boxed{} - 28$

7) $(9 \times 8) + 3 = (9 \times \boxed{}) + 30$

8) $(11 \times 4) + 86 = (9 \times 10) + \boxed{}$

Arithmetic equations can sometimes be in problem form.

Example: What must you multiply by **8** to get an answer which is **half** of **64**?

(half of 64)
$8 \times \boxed{?} = 64 \div 2$
$32 = 32$
Answer: **4**

Exercise 17: 2b Calculate the following:

9) What must **60** be multiplied by to get an answer that is **half** of **480**? _____

10) What must be added to **77** so that it will equal **6** groups of **16**? _____

Score

b. Missing Signs

The equals sign permits a **Missing Sign** to be found. Test different signs to find the correct operation.

Example: Find the missing operation in this equation:

$8\ \boxed{?}\ 9 = 17$ $8\ \boxed{+}\ 9 = 17$ The operation in the box is + because:

(Check it with the inverse operations.) $17 - 9 = 8$
$17 - 8 = 9$

Exercise 17: 3 Calculate the following:

1) $23\ \Box\ 4 = 92$ 2) $13 + 27 = 10\ \Box\ 4$

3) $(189 \div 9) + 7 = 23\ \Box\ 5$ 4) $68\ \Box\ 4 = 17$

5) $11 \times 10 = 61\ \Box\ 49$ 6) $8 \times 17 = 34\ \Box\ 4$

7) $55 - 19 = 2\ \Box\ 18$ 8) $64 \div 8 = 80\ \Box\ 10$

9) $9(1 + 9) + 87 = 43 + 50 + (28\ \Box\ 3)$

10) $(17 \times 3) - (11 + 37) = (4 \times 3)\ \Box\ 9$ Score

© 2018 Stephen Curran

3. Function Machines

Function Machines (also known as Number Machines) are a simple way of representing an equation.

Example: How do function machines relate to equations?

Input Value	**Operations**	**Output Value**
(a number goes into the machine)	(add, subtract, multiply, divide)	(a number comes out of the machine)

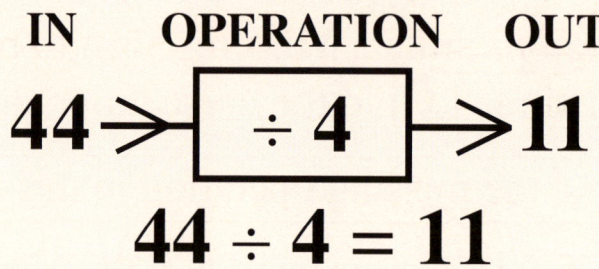

Any input value can be placed in the function machine.

IN   OPERATION   OUT

$44 \rightarrow \boxed{\div 4} \rightarrow 11$

$44 \div 4 = 11$

The output value is equal to the input value with the operational process acting on it. This means the function machine can be viewed as an equation.

a. Finding Output Values

Output Values are discovered by applying the order of operations in which they appear in the function machine.

Example: Find the output value of the machine.

IN   OPERATION   OUT

$3 \rightarrow \boxed{\times 4 + 6} \rightarrow \underline{}$

Multiply by **4** and add **6**

This machine has more than one operation:
$3 \times 4 = 12$ $12 + 6 = 18$

The output value = 18

Tables can show the results of a function machine. Different amounts can be fed into the same function machine with the following results:

In	Out
4	22
8	38
11	50
15	66

Exercise 17: 4 Calculate the following: Score

1) 18 → [÷ 6] → ____ 2) 4 → [× 8 − 10] → ____

3) 81 → [÷ 9 − 8] → ____ 4) 24 → [× 7] → ____

Fill in the function machine before calculating:

5) 22 → [ ] → ____ 6) 28 → [ ] → ____
Multiply by **8** and subtract **16**. Add **20** and divide by **4**.

7) 4 → [− 2 × 11] → ____

8-10) Use the operations − 2 × 11 in this function machine to calculate the three output values in the table:

In	Out
9	____
10	____
18	____

b. Finding Input Values

Input Values are found by using inverse operations:

Add ⟷ Subtract | Multiply ⟷ Divide

Example: Find the input value of the machine.

IN   OPERATION   OUT
? → [× 8 + 2] → 50
⟵ Go backwards

Invert the operations:
Change add to subtract.
Change divide to multiply.

50 − 2 | 48 ÷ 8
= 48 | = 6
Subtract 2 | Divide by 8

The input value = **6**

The table shows more input values found by inverse operations.

In	Out
12 ⟵	98
7 ⟵	58
4 ⟵	34
3 ⟵	26

Exercise 17: 5 Calculate the following:

Score

1) ___ → ÷ 3 → 48   2) ___ → × 10 + 4 → 84

3) ___ → × 11 + 1 → 100   4) ___ → × 7 → 56

Fill in the function machine before calculating:

5) ___ → [ ] → 91   6) ___ → [ ] → 89
   Multiply by **6** and add **19**.   Multiply by **9** and add **17**.

7) ___ → − 5 × 12 → 84

8-10) Use the operations − **5 × 12** in this function machine to calculate the input values in the table:

In	Out
___	60
___	96
___	144

c. Finding Number Operations

A missing operation is found by guessing and testing. Try the operations + − × ÷ in the function machine:

Example: Find the missing operation in the machine.

- As the number is increasing we do not divide or subtract.
- We cannot multiply since there is no multiple that will increase **30** to **80**.
- We must add. The answer can be found by inverting the operation to subtract.

IN   OPERATION   OUT

10 → × 3 ? → 80

Multiply by **3** and **?**

Calculate the first operation. $10 \times 3 = 30$

To find the add, invert and subtract. $80 - 30 = 50$
    $30 \boxed{+ 50} = 80$

The missing operation is: **Add 50**

Exercise 17: 6 Calculate the following: Score

1) 2 → ☐ → 22

2) 46 → +24 → 10

3) 40 → +18 → 23

4) 100 → ☐ → 5

Write in the operations for these machines:

5) 9 → ☐ → 35
Multiply by ? and subtract 19

6) 4 → ☐ → 136
Multiply by 25 and add ?

7-10) Study the function machine below and work out the rule. Then fill in the function machine and the table.

16 → −56 → 8

In	Out
17	___
___	16
20	___

The rule is multiply by _____

4. What is Algebra?

In **Algebra**, letters or symbols called **Variables** represent missing numbers. Italicised lower case (small) letters are normally used from the beginning or end of the alphabet. A same capital and lower case letter represent different amounts.

The letters mostly used in algebra are:

$$a, b, c \text{ and } x, y, z$$

A **Constant** is a value that remains unchanged. It is usually a number. **Terms** are quantities (constants and/or variables) that are linked by + or − signs.

Variable ⟶ $x + 9$ ⟵ Constant

The variable and constant are terms because they are linked by a + sign.

A **Coefficient** is a constant that is associated or connected with a variable. It stands in front of the variable. The value of the variable is multiplied by the coefficient.

$$\text{Coefficient} \longrightarrow 2x \longleftarrow \text{Variable}$$

$2x$ is really $2 \times$ (or times) x So if $x = 7$, the variable **7** is multiplied by the coefficient of **2**.

$$2x \longrightarrow 2 \times 7 = 14$$

If a variable has a coefficient of **1**, it does not have to be included, i.e. $1x = x$

An **Expression** is a collection of quantities made up of constants and variables linked by operation signs such as + and −. It does not include an equals sign. For example,

$$x + y - z$$

Expressions with two or more terms are **Multinomial.**

A multinomial expression with just two terms is **Binomial**. A multinomial expression with three terms is **Trinomial**.

$$x + y \qquad 3 + x^2 - y \qquad 4(x - y)$$
Binomial   **Trinomial**   **Binomial**

'Like Terms' are those terms that are completely identical in respect to their variables and powers. Their coefficients, however, can be different.

'Like Terms' $\longrightarrow$ $2x$ and x $3y^2$ and $2y^2$
  Same variables, coefficients can be different.   Same variables and powers, coefficients can be different.

'Unlike Terms' $\longrightarrow$ x and y $4y$ and $3y^2$
  Different variables.   Same variables but powers must be the same.

An **Algebraic Equation** is a mathematical statement where two expressions (one can be a constant) have equal value.

Binomial Expression → $2x + 3 = 19$ ← Expression (constant only)

Binomial Expression → $2x + 4 = x + 17 - 5$ ← Trinomial Expression

Exercise 17: 7   Answer the following:

Score

Which of these terms: 1) are constants? _____

$3x + 6 - 2y$

2) contain variables? _____

3) show coefficients? _____

4) Is the expression binomial or trinomial? _____

Write whether these terms are like or unlike:

5) $3x$ and $2x$ _____   6) y and y^2 _____   7) b and c _____

8) x^2 and $2x^2$ _____   9) a^2 and $2a$ _____   10) $3z$ and z _____

5. Substitution

Replacing a variable (letter) with a number is called **Substitution**. Substitute the given values for the letters. Expressions are calculated using the order of operations.

Example: If $x = 6$ work out the value of $5(x + 3)$.

$x = 6$ $5(x + 3)$ Substitute 6 for x → $5(6 + 3)$

$= 5 \times 9 = 45$

© 2018 Stephen Curran

Exercise 17: 8

Find the value of these expressions:

Score

If $x = 3; y = 6; z = 9$

1) $3x - y + 2z$
   = _____

2) $x(x - 3) + 2y$
   = _____

3) $2(z - y) + xz$
   = _____

4) $2(2y - x) + z$
   = _____

5) xyz
   = _____

If $a = 5; b = 4; c = 1$

6) $\dfrac{b + c}{a} =$ _____

7) $2a + b$
   = _____

8) $4(b - c)$
   = _____

9) $a^2 + 2b - c$
   = _____

10) $\dfrac{a^2 + 2c^2 - 3}{b(2 + c)} =$ _____

6. More Number Sequences

A **Sequence** is a set of numbers or objects made or written in order, according to a mathematical rule. (See Maths Workbook 1 for introductory work on Number Sequences.) Each value in the sequence is called a term. It is algebra because there are **missing terms** (usually denoted by *n*).

a. Using the Gaps

There is an operational relationship between the numbers. The Four Rules of Number $+ - \times \div$ give the basis for solving all sequences. Look for what is happening in the gaps between the numbers.

Example: What is the rule for this number sequence?

24   21   18   15   12   The next term is: **9**
   3   3   3   3   The rule is: **Minus 3**

1. Numbers may leapfrog over each other and create two sequences, e.g. 3, 2, 6, 4, 9, 6, 12, 8   (3, 6, 9, 12)
   (2, 4, 6, 8)

2. A quick guide to operations:

Adding	- numbers get **bigger slowly**
Multiplying	- numbers get **bigger quickly**
Subtracting	- numbers get **smaller slowly**
Dividing	- numbers get **smaller quickly**

   Note: The multiplying and dividing guides do not apply to fractions (or decimals) which are smaller than 1.

b. Common Number Patterns

Familiarity with certain sequence types can save time. The most common types of sequences are:

Arithmetic Progression - Each new term is made by adding a constant amount to the previous term.

2, 6, 10, 14, 18, 22 Add 4 - next term is **26**

Geometric Progression - Each new term is made by multiplying the previous term by a constant amount.

3, 9, 27, 81 Times by 3 - next term is **243**

Doubling Sequence - Each new term is twice the value of the previous term.

2, 4, 8, 16, 32 Times by 2 - next term is **64**

Fibonacci Sequence - Each new term is made by adding together the previous two terms starting at 1, 1.

1, 1, 2, 3, 5, 8 Add two previous terms - next term is **13**

Lucas Sequence - Each new term is made by adding together the previous two terms starting at 1, 3.

1, 3, 4, 7, 11, 18 Add two previous terms - next term is **29**

Alternating Sequence - Terms are alternately positive and negative. **1, -1, 2, -2, 3, -3** Next term is **4**

Square Numbers (*n*th term is *n²*) **1, 4, 9, 16, 25**
Cube Numbers (*n*th term is *n³*) **1, 8, 27, 64, 125**
Triangular Numbers **1, 3, 6, 10, 15, 21**
Rectangular Numbers **4, 6, 8, 9, 10, 12**
Prime Numbers **2, 3, 5, 7, 11, 13, 17**

Exercise 17: 9   Find the missing terms:

1) **1, 3, 4, 7,** ___ , ___
2) **10, 15, 20, 25,** ___ , ___
3) **100,000, 10,000, 1,000, 100,** ___ , ___
4) **7, 14, 28, 56,** ___ , ___
5) **2, 3, 5, 7,** ___ , ___
6) **1, 8, 27, 64,** ___ , ___
7) **50, 44, 38, 32,** ___ , ___
8) **1, -1, 2, -2,** ___ , ___
9) **1, 4, 9, 16,** ___ , ___
10) **1, 1, 2, 3,** ___ , ___   Score

7. Algebraic Equations
a. Linear Equations

A **Linear Equation** is an equation that only has **first order terms**. This means squared or cubed terms are not used. It is solved by finding the value of the missing number or variable (first order term). They can be written as arithmetic equations, function machines or as algebraic equations.

Example: Show how a linear equation can be written.

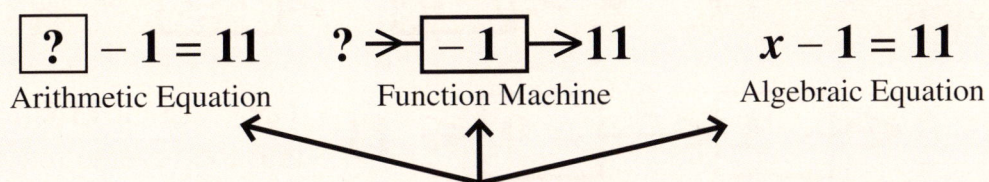

Arithmetic Equation	Function Machine	Algebraic Equation
$\boxed{?} - 1 = 11$	$? \to \boxed{-1} \to 11$	$x - 1 = 11$

Linear equations in an algebraic form replace the missing amount with a variable (letter) such as x or y.

Algebraic linear equations can be solved in three ways:
1) **Reverse Function Machines**.
2) **Reverse Operations**.
3) **Balancing** (doing the same thing to both sides).

b. Reverse Function Machines

Reverse Function Machines can be used algebraically.

Example: Solve $7x - 6 = 50$ with a function machine.

The **variable** x can be fed into a function machine to produce the equation.

IN   OPERATION   OUT

$x \to \boxed{\times 7} \xrightarrow{7x} \boxed{-6} \to 7x - 6$

←———— Go backwards

The **constant 50** is now fed into the reverse machine to give the value of x.

$8 \leftarrow \boxed{\div 7} \xleftarrow{56} \boxed{+6} \leftarrow 50$

$x = 8$ satisfies the equation $7x - 6 = 50$

Exercise 17: 10a   Solve the shaded equations:

1) $\;\boxed{3x + 3 = 27}\;$ $x \to \boxed{\times 3} \xrightarrow{3x} \boxed{+3} \to 3x + 3$

      ___ $\leftarrow \boxed{\div 3} \xleftarrow{24} \boxed{-3} \leftarrow 27$ The constant **27** is fed into the reverse machine.

© 2018 Stephen Curran

2) $\dfrac{a}{3} + 9 = 11$ $a \to \boxed{\div 3} \xrightarrow{\frac{a}{3}} \boxed{+9} \to \dfrac{a}{3}+9$

___ $\leftarrow \boxed{\times 3} \xleftarrow{2} \boxed{-9} \leftarrow 11$ The constant **11** is fed into the reverse machine.

3) $5y + 4 = 24$ ___ $\leftarrow \boxed{\div 5} \xleftarrow{20} \boxed{-4} \leftarrow 24$

4) $7a - 2 = 19$ ___ $\leftarrow \boxed{} \leftarrow \boxed{} \leftarrow 19$

5) $\dfrac{x-6}{5} = 3$ ___ $\leftarrow \boxed{} \leftarrow \boxed{} \leftarrow 3$

c. Reverse Operations

Reverse Operations can solve algebraic equations.

Example: Solve $\dfrac{x}{3} + 7 = 19$ with reverse operations.

The objective is to get *x* on its own on one side of the equation. When a term is moved to the other side its sign changes. Inverse operations apply:

- Add ⟷ Subtract
- Multiply ⟷ Divide

To get the *x* term on its own, move all constants to the opposite side.

$\dfrac{x}{3} + 7 = 19$ Turn the + 7 to − 7 by changing sides.

$\dfrac{x}{3} = 19 \, (-7)$

$\dfrac{x}{3} = 12$ Turn the ÷ 3 to × 3 by changing sides.

$x = 12 \, (\times 3)$

$x = 36$

© 2018 Stephen Curran

Exercise 17: 10b Solve these equations:

6) $\dfrac{x}{7} - 4 = 13$

   $x = \underline{}$

7) $4x - 6 = 38$

   $x = \underline{}$

8) $16 = 5y - 9$

   This equation is round the other way. Leave *y* on the right instead of bringing it to the left, then do the equation in the same way.

   $y = \underline{}$

9) $15 = 4a - 5$

   $a = \underline{}$

10) $6b + 9 = 21$

   $b = \underline{}$

Score

d. Balancing

The **Balancing Method** requires the unknown value to be left on one side of the equation and constants added or subtracted, as required, to make them equal to **0** on this side. The = sign acts like a weighing scale. **Whatever action is carried out on one side must be done to the other side.**

Example: Find the value of *x* if $3x - 1 = 32$

Equations require adding and subtracting to be done before multiplying and dividing.

1. Deal with add/subtract first. Add **1** to cancel the **− 1**.

2. Add **1** to **32** on the other side.

$3x - 1 = 32$

Add 1 to both sides.

$3x \overset{+1}{-} 1 = 32 \overset{+1}{}$

$3x = 32 + 1$

3. **$3x$** is really **$3 \times x$**. To get **x** alone we divide **$3x$** by **3**.

   Divide both sides by 3.
   $$\frac{3x}{3} = 33 \quad ^{\div 3}$$

4. Divide **33** by **3** to find the value of **x**.
   $$x = \frac{33}{3}$$

5. **x** is now on its own.
   $$x = 11$$

Exercise 17: 11a Solve these equations:

1) $6x + 10 = 82$

   $x = $ _____

2) $5x - 12 = 23$

   $x = $ _____

3) $\frac{x}{7} + 9 = 6$

   $x = $ _____

4) $3x + 4 = 19$

   $x = $ _____

e. Variables on Both Sides

Equations with more than one variable either side can be solved in a similar way. The rule is 'get rid of the smallest letter term by moving it to the other side of the equals sign'.

Example: Find the value of $6x + 1 = 2x - 15$

If an equation has two same type variables these must be combined first.

Two Variables
$$6x + 1 = 2x - 15$$

1. Cancel **2x** by subtracting. $6x + 1 = \cancel{2x} - 15$
   $_{-2x}$

2. Balance by placing
   -2x on the other side. $6x - 2x + 1 = -15$

3. Subtract the two letter
   terms **6x − 2x** to give **4x**. $4x + 1 = -15$

4. Cancel **+1** by subtracting **1**
   to the same side. $4x \cancel{+1}^{-1} = -15$

5. Balance it by subtracting **1**
   from the other side. $4x = -15 - 1$

6. Subtract **1** from **-15** to find **4x**. $4x = -16$

7. Divide **x** by **4** to find **x**. $\dfrac{x}{4} = -16$

8. Divide **-16** by **4** to find **x**. $x = -4$

Exercise 17: 11b   Solve these equations:

5) $x + 6 = 28 - x$ 6) $3y + 10 = 50 - 7y$

x = ____   y = ____

7) $4x + 8 = 5x + 19$ 8) $5y - 6 = 58 - 3y$

x = ____   y = ____

9) $4x + 5 = x + 50$ 10) $2 - 6x = 47 - x$

$x = $ _____ $x = $ _____

Score

f. Equations with Brackets

If equations have brackets, multiply them out and solve the equation as usual.

$$3(5x - 10) = 3(x + 6)$$

$3(5x - 10)$
$3 \times 5x = 15x$
$3 \times 10 = 30$

$3(x + 6)$
$3 \times x = 3x$
$3 \times 6 = 18$

$$15x - 30 = 3x + 18$$

Exercise 17: 12a   Solve these equations:

1) $3(3x + 4) = 3$ 2) $6(2y + 3) = 5(4y - 6)$

$x = $ _____ $y = $ _____

3) $4(6x - 2) = 8(2x + 1)$ 4) $3(4x - 5) = 81$

$x = $ _____ $x = $ _____

5) $3(2y + 5) = 5(y + 2)$ 6) $2(x + 1) = x + 6$

$y = $ _____ $x = $ _____

f. Equations with Brackets

Example: Substitute the solution into $6x - 10 = 2x + 2$.

1. The solution to this equation is 3.
2. Substitute 3 into the equation.
3. The equation balances.

$$6x - 10 = 2x + 2$$
$$x = 3$$
$$(6 \times 3) - 10 = (2 \times 3) + 2$$
$$8 = 8$$

Exercise 17: 12b Solve these equations:

Score

7) $5a - 10 = 2a + 5$ 9) $4x - 5 = 3x + 3$

$a = $ _____ $x = $ _____

Substitute into the equations to check they work:

8) $5a - 10 = 2a + 5$ 10) $4x - 5 = 3x + 3$

____ = ____   ____ = ____

It balances? Yes or no? ____   It balances? Yes or no? ____

h. More Equations

More difficult equations often combine the use of brackets, fractions and negative numbers.

Example: Calculate $8(1 + \frac{x}{4}) = 24$

1. Divide both sides. $(1 + \frac{x}{4}) = 24 \div 8$
   $(1 + \frac{x}{4}) = 3$
2. Subtract **1** and then multiply both sides by **4**.
   $\frac{x}{4} = 2$
   $x = 8$

Exercise 17: 13   Solve these equations:

1) $\frac{x}{2} + 1 = -9$ 2) $8(y + \frac{1}{4}) = 18$

$x =$ ____ $y =$ ____

Now try these more complex equations on paper:

3) $\frac{z + 10}{4} = 5$ 4) $2(3c - 2) - 10 = -8$

$z =$ ____ $c =$ ____

5) $6(2x - 3) + 3(x + 7) = 18$ $x =$ ____

6) $\frac{7y - 9}{4} = 10$ 7) $\frac{3x - 10}{5} = 4$

$y =$ ____ $x =$ ____

8) $2(2x - 6) - 3(x + 8) = 16$ $x =$ ____

9) $2(2x + 3) = 3(2x - 3)$ $x =$ ____

10) $\frac{1}{2}(z - 2) = z + 8$ $z =$ ____

Score

8. Algebraic Formulae
a. What is a Formula?

A **Formula** is a mathematical rule, usually written as an equation. If a number is substituted into the formula it will be changed into another number by mathematical operations.

For example, the formula for the area of a rectangle is:
Area = Length × Width

Algebraic Formulae are equations that also state a rule that can either be applied generally or just to a particular question. They use **symbols** or **letters** to denote the missing variable. Many formulae can be stated in an algebraic form.

For example, a formula for the perimeter of a square is:
P = 4L (Perimeter = 4 × Length of one side.)

b. Turning Words into Formulae

Statements or expressions can be converted into formulae. The Four Rules of Number $+ - \times \div$ provide the basis.

The most common statements for creating formulae from the Four Rules of Number are listed below:

Addition	Subtraction
more than; on top of; increased by; added to; plus	is taken away; from; decreased by; reduced; is removed; less than

Example 1:
What is **n increased by 4?**

$n + 4$ or $4 + n$

This can be written in two ways because addition is commutative.

Example 2:
What is **n reduced by 4?**

$n - 4$

This cannot be written as $4 - n$ because subtraction is not commutative.

Multiplication

increased by a factor of;
tripled;   doubled;
lots of;   quadrupled

Example 3:
What is **4 lots of n?**

$n4$ or $4n$

This can be written in two ways since multiplication is commutative.

Division

reduced by a factor of;
shared out;   divided up;
halved;   split between

Example 4:
What is **4 divided into n?** → $\frac{4}{n}$

This cannot be written as $\frac{n}{4}$ because division is not commutative.

Exercise 17: 14   Write as expressions:

1) **3** less than **z** _____

2) **8** more than **5** lots of **x** _____

3) **b** decreased by **3** _____

4) **10** more than **c** _____

5) Twice **p** minus **r** _____

6) **a** split between **5** _____

7) Double **b**, take away **5** shared between **4** _____

8) **y** halved plus **z** _____

9) **9** added to **y**, shared between **x** _____

10) **p** increased by **3** then divided up by **n** _____

Score

c. Formulaic Expressions

Formulae can be used to represent and solve problems. Look out for the Four Rules of Number $+ - \times \div$

Example: Shauna scored m marks in maths, n marks in NVR and v marks in VR. What was Shauna's total mark?

Shauna's total mark was $m + n + v$

Exercise 17: 15a Write as algebraic expressions:

1) A bag of x sweets is shared among 3 children. How many sweets does each child receive? _____ sweets.

2) A piece of ribbon measures y metres and is cut into 8 equal lengths. Each piece measures _____ metres.

3) Georgia takes her dog for a walk everyday before and after school. Each walk is x miles long. On Saturday and Sunday she takes her dog for a longer walk of y miles. How many miles does she walk in one week? _____ miles.

4) 84 children are taken on a school trip. Each child takes £x for lunch and £y for entrance. What is the total amount taken by the group? _____ pounds.

5) Blake earns x pounds each week from his Saturday job. He also gets y pounds pocket money each month from his parents. How much does Blake get in one year? _____ pounds.

d. Formulaic Equations

Sentences can be written as equations if their wording requires an equals sign.

is; total; is the same as; gives the same answer as; find; find the answer to

Example: A family of four hire bicycles for the day whilst on holiday. The bicycles cost **£7** for the first **2** hours, then an hourly rate of **£1.30** for each additional hour (**h**).
Write down the formula (in pence) for the cost (**c**) of hiring the bicycles.

The equation can be expressed as: $c = 700 + 130h$ for the cost of one person. If amounts are supplied the equation offers a solution:

How much would it cost the family to hire the bicycles for **5** hours?

$c = 700 + 130h$

$c = 700 + (130 \times 5)$

$c = 700 + 650$

$c = 1350$

For the cost of four people (**4c**).

$4c = 1350 \times 4$

$= 5400p$ or £54

Exercise 17: 15b Write and solve as equations:

6) To find **y**, square **x**, double this and add **8**.

   a) Equation: $y =$ _____

   b) If **x** is **2** find **y**. _____

7) There are **22** children in a class and they divide themselves into **3** equal teams (each with **x** children) for sports. There are **4** who arrive too late to play.

   a) The equation is: _____

   b) How many children are in each team? _____

8) An ice cream van sells ice cream cones and ice lollies. An ice cream cone costs **90p** and an ice lolly costs **50p**. The total (T) is found using the equation:

$T = 90c + 50l$ c = ice cream cone l = ice lolly

a) Week 1 $c = 20$ and $l = 16$, so T is _____

b) Week 2 $T = 3140$ and $c = 21$, so l is ____

9) If x stickers cost **80p**:

a) Write down a formula to the cost (c) in pence of one sticker. _____

b) What is the cost of **20** stickers? _____

Questions are more complex if the equation has to be created from two binomial expressions.

Example: | Write this sentence as an algebraic equation:
Geoffrey worked out that if he took his age (a), multiplied it by **3** and added **7**, it would give the same answer as adding **27** to his age.

If the age was a, multiplying it by **3** and adding **7** would give the expression: $3a + 7$:

Adding **27** to the age (a) gives: $a + 27$

Equating these expressions gives: $3a + 7 = a + 27$

This can now be solved: $3a + 7 = a + 27$

$$3a = a + 20$$
$$2a = 20$$
$$a = 10 \text{ years}$$

Exercise 17: 15c Find and solve the equation:

10) Olivia found out that if she multiplied the number of trading cards (*x*) she had by **6** and subtracted **4**, it was the same as if she added **16** to the number of cards.
   a) Equation: _____ = _____
   b) Solution: *x* = _____

Score

e. Formulae and Shapes
(i) Perimeter

Perimeter Formula can be expressed algebraically.

Example: Find the perimeter of a rectangle **3*x*** centimetres long and (***x* + 8**) centimetres wide.

1. Add the length of all the sides.
   $(x + 8) + 3x + (x + 8) + 3x$
2. Simplify into bracket form.
   $8x + 16$
   ↓
   $8(x + 2)$cm

Divide both numbers by the highest common factor (HCF), which is 8.

$8x ÷ 8 = x$
$16 ÷ 8 = 2$

x + 8
3*x*

Answer: $8x + 16 = 8(x + 2)$cm

Exercise 17: 16a Write as formulae:

1) Write the perimeter of this equilateral triangle as an algebraic expression.

   _____

   x + 1

2) Write the perimeter of this shape as a formula:

   Perimeter = _____

   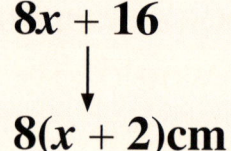

3) What is the perimeter of this shape?

   Perimeter = _____ cm

   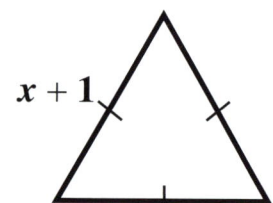

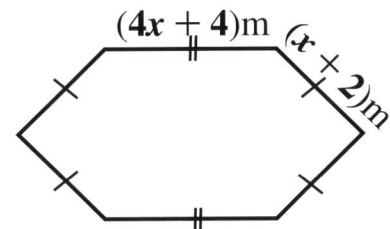

4) The perimeter of this shape can be written as:

Set out: _____

Simplify: _____ m

(ii) Area

The **Area** of shapes can also be written algebraically:

Area of a Rectangle = Length × Width   **Area = L × W**

Example: Calculate the area of a rectangle $(7x + 8)$ metres long and $2x$ metres wide.

Area = Length × Width
Area = $(7x + 8) \times 2x$
Area = $(14x^2 + 16x)$ m²

Note: $x \times x = x^2$

It is better to write square metres in full to avoid confusion as the x value has also been squared.

Area of the Rectangle = $(14x^2 + 16x)$ square metres

Exercise 17: 16b   Write as formulae:

5) What is the formula for the area of this shape?

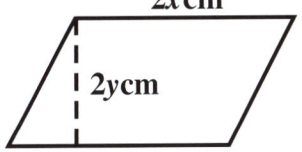

a) xy^2 b) $x^2 + y^2$

c) $4xy$ d) $x^2 - y^2$

6) Write the area for the rectangle $(3x - 10)$ metres in length and $5x$ metres in width.

Area = _____ square metres

7) Write the area for the triangle.
   Area = _____

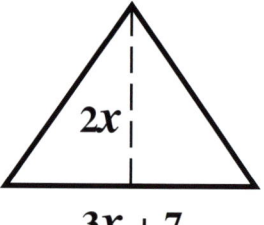

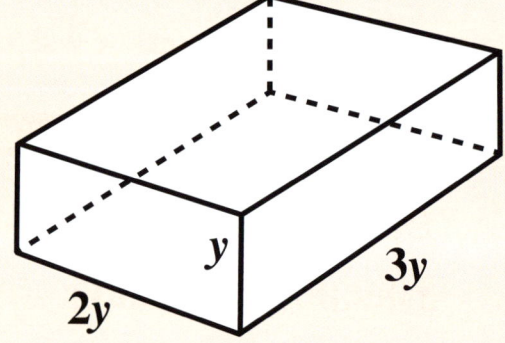

8) One side of the square is *a*cm. Write the area and perimeter as formulae:
   a) Area = _____
   b) Perimeter = _____

9) The length of a carpet is **5** times its width. The width is *x* + **3** metres. The formula for the area is:
   a) Area = _____
   b) Perimeter = _____

(iii) Volume

The **Volume** of a Cuboid = Length × Width × Height

Example: Find the volume of a cuboid **3y** metres long, **2y** metres wide and **y** metres high.

Volume = **L × W × H**

Volume = **3y × 2y × y** = **6y³m³**

Note: $y \times y \times y = y^3$
It is better to write cubic metres in full to avoid confusion as the *y* value has also been cubed.

Volume of the cuboid = **6y³ cubic metres**

Exercise 17: 16c Write as formulae:

10)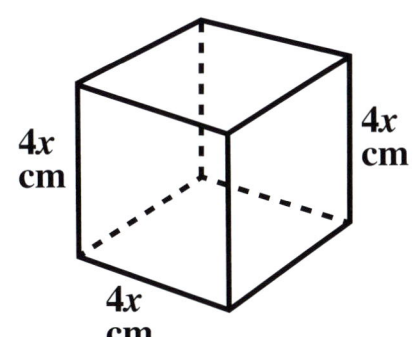

Volume of the cube = _____ cubic centimetres

9. Algebra Problems

Exercise 17: 17 Answer the following:

1) Write the perimeter of this shape as an algebraic expression.
   _____

2) Solve this equation: $5(3x - 2) = 6 - x$ $x = $ ____

3) Piers counted the money in his piggy bank. He found that if he took the amount of money he has (m), multiplied it by **6** and then subtracted **17**, he would get the same amount as if he counted the money he had and added **25** pounds. The equation is: _____

4) Here is a pattern of number pairs:

a	b
1	8
2	13
3	18
4	23

Complete the rule of the number pattern.

$b = $ ____ $\times a + $ ____

5) 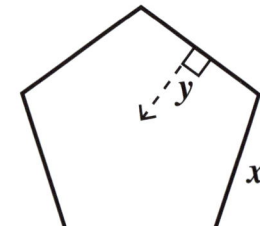 Calculate the area of this shape.

Area = _____

6) Cooking instructions for a roast beef dinner:
Allow **30mins** cooking time for each kilogram of meat (**w**) plus an extra **40mins**. Write a formula for the total time taken (**T**) to cook the roast. How long would it take to cook a **2kg** beef joint? _____mins

7) Solve **5x + 9 = 64** with a function machine.

x = _____   x ➤ ×5 ➤ +9 ➤ 64

8) 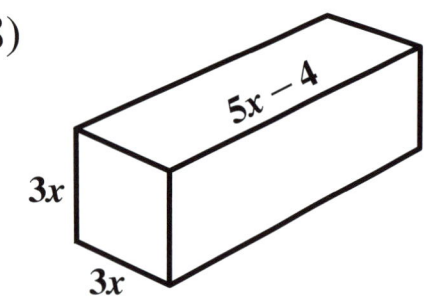 Find the volume of this cuboid.

Volume = _____

9) Four people run a cake stall at a school fete. Amira sells a cakes. Macey sells **7** more cakes than Amira. Izzy sells **4** times as many cakes as Amira. Larry sells **8** less cakes than Izzy. Write down on the table how many cakes each person sold using algebraic expression.

Name	Cakes sold
Amira	a
Macey	
Izzy	
Larry	

10) a) Solve the equation **6x + 4 = 22**. x = _____

b) Using this value of **x**, solve the evaluate the expression:
7x − 9 = _____

Answers

KS2 Maths
Year 5/6 Workbook 5

Chapter Sixteen
Tables, Charts, Graphs and Diagrams

Exercise 16: 1a
1) £12
2) a) 489mm
   b) 407mm

Exercise 16: 1b
3) a) 30 miles
   b) 48 miles
   c) 73 miles
   d) 460 miles
4) a) 66km
   b) 333km
   c) 327km
   d) 655km

Exercise 16: 1c
5) a) Saifa and Pheobe
   b) Abygael
   c) Saifa
6) a) Marco
   b) Thomas
   c) 2 people

Exercise 16: 1d
7) coat = 6; glasses = 3; book = 5; football = 3; bag = 5; Total = 22

Exercise 16: 1e

8)
Times	Tally	Fr
1-15	⊦⊦⊦⊦ I	6
16-30	IIII	4
31-45	⊦⊦⊦⊦ I	6
46-60	IIII	4
Total	⊦⊦⊦⊦ ⊦⊦⊦⊦ ⊦⊦⊦⊦ ⊦⊦⊦⊦	20

9)
Marks	Tally	Fr
1-2	III	3
3-4	IIII	4
5-6	III	3
7-8	⊦⊦⊦⊦	5
9-10	⊦⊦⊦⊦ I	6
Total	⊦⊦⊦⊦ ⊦⊦⊦⊦ ⊦⊦⊦⊦ ⊦⊦⊦⊦ I	21

10)
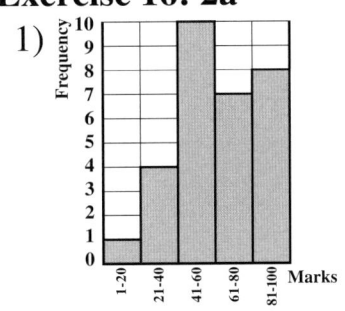

Weight (w)	Tally	Fr
20 - 25	I	1
26 - 30	IIII	4
31 - 35	⊦⊦⊦⊦	5
36 - 40	⊦⊦⊦⊦ II	7
41 - 45	III	3
Total	⊦⊦⊦⊦ ⊦⊦⊦⊦ ⊦⊦⊦⊦ ⊦⊦⊦⊦	20

Exercise 16: 2a
1) [histogram]

2) a) 214 tickets
   b) Wednesday
   c) 22 tickets
3) a) 30 children
   b) 11 children
   c) True
4) a) Team E
   b) 5 points
   c) 5 points
5) a) January
   b) 145mm
   c) 990mm
   d) 82.5mm

Exercise 16: 2b
6) a) $1/6$
   b) 10
   c) 25%
   d) 90°
7) a) 3 hours
   b) 3 hours
   c) 3 hours
   d) 3 hours
   e) 24 hours
8) a) 15
   b) 15
   c) 10
   d) 60

9) a) 5
   b) 10
   c) 5
   d) 5
   e) 5
10) a) 15
    b) 30
    c) 15
    d) 15
    e) 15

Exercise 16: 3
1) Monday
2) Friday
3) 9°C
4) 25°C
5) Tuesday & Wednesday
6)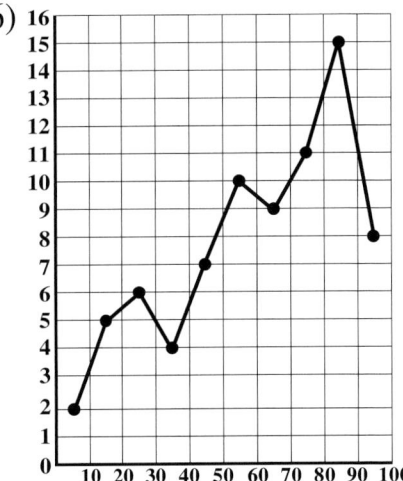
7) 77
8) 81-90
9) 1-10
10) 53

Exercise 16: 4
1) 30
2) Marian
3) Zainab
4) 6
5) Isobella
6) Monday

KS2 Maths
Year 5/6 Workbook 5

Answers

7) Sunday
8) Saturday
9) Monday
10) 69 hours

Exercise 16: 5
1-7)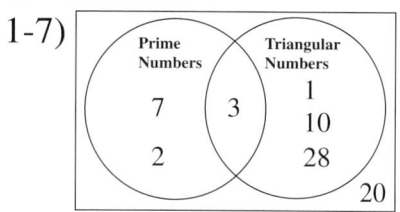

8) 3
9) 20
10) 2 & 7

Exercise 16: 6
1-8)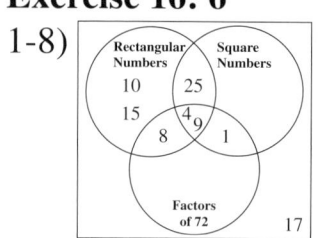

9) 10 & 15
10) 17

Exercise 16: 7
1-10)

	Multiples of 3	Multiples of 7
Odd	9, 15, 27	35, 49
Even	12, 36	14, 28, 70

Exercise 16: 8
1-10)

	Prime	Not Prime
Factors of 40	2, 5	4, 8, 10, 20, 40
Factors of 21	3, 7	21

Exercise 16: 9a
1) ×10
2)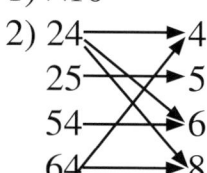
3) squared
4) 3 → 9
   4 → 11
   7 → 17
   8 → 19
5) cubed; 125
6) -3; 97

Exercise 16: 9b
7) a) 20 years
   b) nephew
   c) sister
   d) 19 years
8) a) cone
   b) hexagon
   c) true

Exercise 16: 9c
9) Stephan
10) a) 31 years
    b) 11 years

Exercise 16: 10
1) a) 5   b) 20
   c) 10   d) 15
   e) 10
2) 24
3) 1
4) 8
5)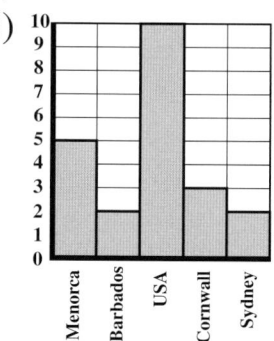

Answers

KS2 Maths
Year 5/6 Workbook 5

6) is it clean?
7) 36
8)

	Factors of 12	Factors of 40
Odd	3	5
Even	6 12	8 10 20 40

9) a) Ireland
   b) 2
   c) Japan
10) a) 43 miles
    b) 69 miles
    c) 146 miles

Chapter Seventeen
Algebra
Exercise 17: 1
1) 82
2) 2
3) 196
4) 100
5) 199
6) 76
7) 54
8) 37
9) 28
10) 43

Exercise 17: 2a
1) 33
2) 16
3) 14
4) 30
5) 74
6) 29
7) 5
8) 40

Exercise 17: 2b
9) 4
10) 19

Exercise 17: 3
1) ×
2) ×
3) +
4) ÷
5) +
6) ×
7) ×
8) ÷
9) ×
10) −

Exercise 17: 4
1) 3
2) 22
3) 1
4) 168
5) 160
6) 12
7) 22
8) 77
9) 88
10) 176

Exercise 17: 5
1) 144
2) 8
3) 9
4) 8
5) 12
6) 8
7) 12
8) 10
9) 13
10) 17

Exercise 17: 6
1) ×11 or + 20
2) + 24 ÷ 7 or + 24 − 60

3) ÷ 8 + 18 or − 35 + 18
4) ÷ 20 or − 95
5) 6
6) 36
7) 4
   Rule is multiply by 4 and subtract 56
8) 12
9) 18
10) 24

Exercise 17: 7
1) 6
2) $3x$ and $-2y$
3) $3x$ and $-2y$
4) trinomial
5) like
6) unlike
7) unlike
8) like
9) unlike
10) like

Exercise 17: 8
1) 21   2) 12
3) 33   4) 27
5) 162 6) 1
7) 14   8) 12
9) 32   10) 2

Exercise 17: 9
1) 11, 18
2) 30, 35
3) 10, 1
4) 112, 224
5) 11, 13
6) 125, 216
7) 26, 20
8) 3, -3
9) 25, 36
10) 5, 8

KS2 Maths
Year 5/6 Workbook 5

Answers

Exercise 17: 10a
1) 8   2) 6
3) 4   4) 3
5) 21

Exercise 17: 10b
6) 119   7) 11
8) 5   9) 5
10) 2

Exercise 17: 11a
1) 12   2) 7
3) -21   4) 5

Exercise 17: 11b
5) $x = 11$
6) $y = 4$
7) $x = -11$
8) $y = 8$
9) $x = 15$
10) $x = -9$

Exercise 17: 12a
1) $x = -1$
2) $y = 6$
3) $x = 2$
4) $x = 8$
5) $y = -5$
6) $x = 4$

Exercise 17: 12b
7) $a = 5$
8) $15 = 15$
   yes it balances
9) $x = 8$
10) $27 = 27$
   yes it balances

Exercise 17: 13
1) $x = -20$
2) $y = 2$
3) $z = 10$
4) $c = 1$

5) $x = 1$
6) $y = 7$
7) $x = 10$
8) $x = 52$
9) $x = 7\frac{1}{2}$
10) $z = -18$

Exercise 17: 14
1) $z - 3$
2) $5x + 8$
3) $b - 3$
4) $c + 10$
5) $2p - r$
6) $\dfrac{a}{5}$
7) $\dfrac{2b - 5}{4}$
8) $\dfrac{y}{2} + z$
9) $\dfrac{y + 9}{x}$
10) $\dfrac{p + 3}{n}$

Exercise 17: 15a
1) $\dfrac{x}{3}$
2) $\dfrac{y}{8}$
3) $10x + 2y$
4) $84(x + y)$
5) $52x + 12y$

Exercise 17: 15b
6) a) $2x^2 + 8$
   b) 16
7) a) $3x + 4 = 22$
   b) 6
8) a) 2600
   b) 25
9) a) $c = \dfrac{80}{x}$
   b) $\dfrac{80}{x} \times 20$

Exercise 17: 15c
10) a) $6x - 4 = x + 16$
    b) $x = 4$

Exercise 17: 16a
1) $3(x + 1)$
2) $2(7x + 11)$
3) $2(a + b)$
4) $4(3x + 4)$

Exercise 17: 16b
5) c) $4xy$
6) $15x^2 - 50x$ or $5x(3x - 10)$
7) $3x^2 + 7x$ or $x(3x + 7)$
8) a) a^2
   b) $4a$
9) a) $(x + 3)(5x + 15)$ or
      $5x^2 + 30x + 45$ or $5(x + 3)^2$
   b) $12(x + 3)$

Exercise 17: 16c
10) $64x^3$

Exercise 17: 17
1) $13x + 12$
2) $x = 1$
3) $6m - 17 = m + 25$
4) $b = 5 \times a + 3$
5) Area $= \dfrac{5xy}{2}$
6) 100 mins
7) $x = 11$
8) Volume $= 45x^3 - 36x^2$
   or $9x^2(5x - 4)$

9)

Name	Cakes sold
Amira	a
Macey	$a + 7$
Izzy	$4a$
Larry	$4a - 8$

10) a) $x = 3$
    b) 12

PROGRESS CHARTS

Shade in your score for each exercise on the graph. Add up for your total score. If there are a) b) c) etc. parts to a question, all parts must be correct to gain a mark.

16. TABLES, CHARTS, GRAPHS & DIAGRAMS

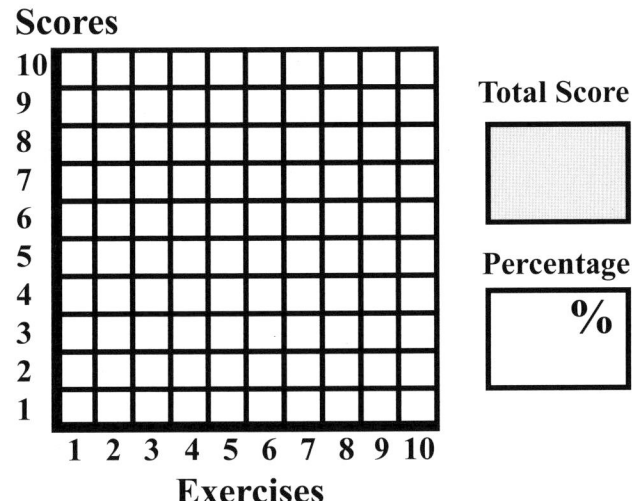

17. ALGEBRA

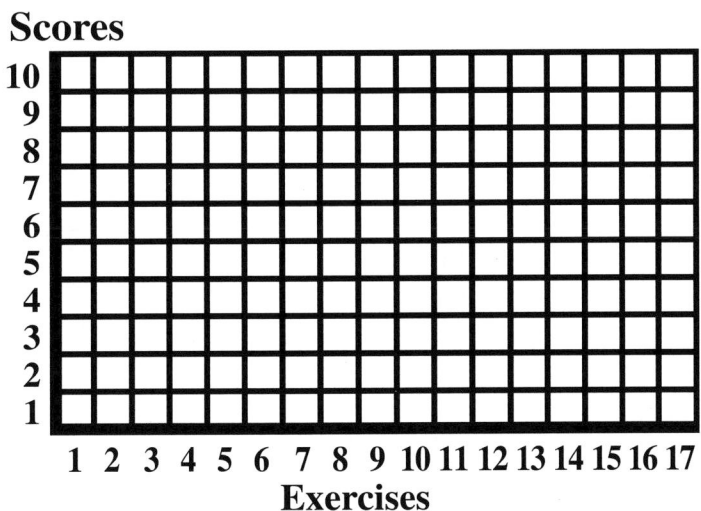

For the average add up % and divide by 2

Overall Percentage ____ %

CERTIFICATE OF ACHIEVEMENT

This certifies

_____

has successfully completed

KS2 Maths
Year 5/6
WORKBOOK 5

Overall percentage score achieved [ ] %

Comment _____

_____

Signed _____
(teacher/parent/guardian)

Date _____